Study Guide to Accompany

The Human Body in Health & Disease

Custom Version

6th Edition

Prepared by Linda Swisher, RN, EdD

3251 Riverport Lane
St. Louis, Missouri 63043

STUDY GUIDE TO ACCOMPANY THE HUMAN BODY IN HEALTH   ISBN: 978-0-323-28051-8
& DISEASE CUSTOM VERSION, 6TH EDITION

Notices

Knowledge and best practice in this field are constantly changing. As new research and experience broaden our understanding, changes in research methods, professional practices, or medical treatment may become necessary.

Practitioners and researchers must always rely on their own experience and knowledge in evaluating and using any information, methods, compounds, or experiments described herein. In using such information or methods they should be mindful of their own safety and the safety of others, including parties for whom they have a professional responsibility.

With respect to any drug or pharmaceutical products identified, readers are advised to check the most current information provided (i) on procedures featured or (ii) by the manufacturer of each product to be administered, to verify the recommended dose or formula, the method and duration of administration, and contraindications. It is the responsibility of practitioners, relying on their own experience and knowledge of their patients, to make diagnoses, to determine dosages and the best treatment for each individual patient, and to take all appropriate safety precautions.

To the fullest extent of the law, neither the Publisher nor the authors, contributors, or editors assume any liability for any injury and/or damage to persons or property as a matter of products liability, negligence or otherwise, or from any use or operation of any methods, products, instructions, or ideas contained in the material herein.

ISBN: 978-0-323-28051-8

Vice President and Content Strategy Director: Linda Duncan
Executive Content Strategist: Kellie White
Content Development Specialist: Joe Gramlich
Content Coordinator: Nathan Wurm-Cutter
Publishing Services Manager: Catherine Jackson
Project Manager: Rhoda Bontrager

Printed in the United States of America

Last digit is the print number: 9 8 7 6 5 4 3 2 1

**Working together to grow
libraries in developing countries**

www.elsevier.com | www.bookaid.org | www.sabre.org

ELSEVIER   BOOK AID International   Sabre Foundation

Acknowledgments

I wish to express my appreciation to the staff of Elsevier, Inc., especially Kellie White, Joe Gramlich, Catherine Jackson, and Rhoda Bontrager for opening the door and assisting me with this text. My continued admiration and gratitude to Kevin Patton for another outstanding edition of *The Human Body in Health & Disease*. Your time and dedication to science education will hopefully inspire potential caregivers and improve the quality of health care for the future.

To Bill, who is always there, my thanks for the whispers of inspiration and encouragement.

Finally, to the designer of the human body, this book is dedicated. What a miraculous creation!

Linda Swisher, RN, EdD

Preface

TO THE INSTRUCTOR

This Study Guide is designed to help your students master basic anatomy and physiology. It works in two ways.

First, the section of the preface titled "To the Student" contains detailed instructions on:

- How to achieve good grades in anatomy and physiology
- How to read the textbook
- How to use the exercises in this Study Guide
- How to use visual memory as a learning tool
- How to use mnemonic devices as learning aids
- How to prepare for an examination
- How to take an examination
- How to find out why questions were missed on an examination

Second, the Study Guide itself contains features that facilitate learning:

1. LEARNING OBJECTIVES, designed to break down the process of learning into small units. The questions in this Study Guide have been developed to help the student master the learning objectives identified at the beginning of each chapter in the text. The Guide is also sequenced to correspond to key areas of each chapter. A variety of questions has been prepared to cover the material effectively and expose the student to multiple learning approaches.

2. CROSSWORD PUZZLES, to encourage the use of new vocabulary words and emphasize the proper spelling of these terms.

3. OPTIONAL APPLICATION QUESTIONS, particularly targeted for the health occupations student but appropriate for any student of anatomy and physiology because questions are based entirely on information contained within the chapter.

4. DIAGRAMS with key features marked by numbers for identification. Students can easily check their work by comparing the diagram in the workbook with the equivalent figure in the text.

5. PAGE NUMBER REFERENCES in the answer section. Each answer is cross-referenced to the appropriate text page. In addition, questions are grouped into specific topics that correspond to the text. Each major topic of the Study Guide provides references to specific areas of the text, so that students having difficulty with a particular grouping of questions have a specific reference area to assist them with remedial work. This is of great assistance to both instructor and student, because remedial work is made easier and more effective when the area of weakness is identified accurately.

These features should make mastery of the material a rewarding experience for both instructor and student.

TO THE STUDENT

How to Achieve Good Grades in Anatomy and Physiology

This Study Guide is designed to help you be successful in learning anatomy and physiology. Before you begin using the Study Guide, read the following suggestions. Successful students understand effective study techniques and have good study habits.

How to Read the Textbook

Keep up with the reading assignments. Read the textbook assignment before the instructor covers the material in a lecture. If you have failed to read the assignment beforehand, you may not grasp what the instructor is talking about in the lecture. When you read, do the following:

1. As you finish reading a sentence, ask yourself if you understand it. If you do not, put a question mark in the margin by that sentence. If the instructor does not clarify the material in lecture, ask him or her to explain it to you further.

2. Do the learning objectives in the text. A learning objective is a specific task that you are expected to be able to do after you have read a chapter. It sets specific goals for the student and breaks down learning into small units. It emphasizes the key points that the author is making in the chapter.

3. Underline and make notes in the margin to highlight key ideas, mark something you need to reinforce at a later time, or indicate things that you do not understand.

4. If you come to a word you do not understand, look it up in a dictionary. Write the word on one side of an index card and its definition on the other side. Carry these cards with you, and when you have a spare minute, use them like flash cards. If you do not know how to spell or pronounce a word, you will have a difficult time remembering it.

5. Carefully study each diagram and illustration as you read. Many students ignore these aids. The author included them to help students understand the material.

6. Summarize what you read. After finishing a paragraph, try to restate the main ideas. Do this again when you finish the chapter. Identify and mentally restate the main concepts of the chapter. Check to see if you are correct. In short, be an active reader. Do not just stare at a page or read it superficially.

7. Finally, attack each unit of learning with a positive mental attitude. Motivation and perseverance are prime factors in achieving good grades. The combination of your instructor, the text, the Study Guide, and your dedicated work will lead to success in anatomy and physiology.

How to Use the Exercises in This Study Guide

After you have read a chapter and learned all of the new words, begin working with the Study Guide. Read the overview of the chapter, which summarizes the main points.

Familiarize yourself with the "Topics for Review" section, which emphasizes the learning objectives outlined in the text. Complete the questions and diagrams in the Study Guide. After completing the exercises in a chapter, you can check your answers in the back of the book. Each answer is referenced to the appropriate text page. Additionally, questions are grouped into specific topics that correspond to the text. Each major topic of the Study Guide provides references to specific areas of the text, so if you are having difficulty with a particular grouping of questions, you have a specific reference area to assist you with remedial work. This feature allows you to identify your area of weakness accurately. A variety of questions is offered throughout the Study Guide to help you cover the material effectively. The following examples are among the exercises that have been included to assist you.

Multiple Choice Questions

Multiple choice questions will have only one correct answer for you to select from the several possibilities presented. There are two types of multiple choice questions that you need to be acquainted with:

1. "None of the above is correct" questions. These questions test your ability to recall rather than recognize the correct answer. You would select the "none of the above" choice only if all the other choices in that particular question were incorrect.

2. Sequence questions. These questions test your ability to arrange a list of structures in the correct order. In this type of question, you are asked to determine the sequence of the structures given in the various choices, and then you are to select the structure listed that would be third in that sequence, as in this example:

Which one of the following structures is the third through which food passes?
A. Stomach
B. Mouth
C. Large intestine
D. Esophagus
E. Anus

The correct answer is *A*.

Matching Questions

Matching questions ask the student to select the correct answer from a list of terms and to write that answer in the space provided.

True or False Questions

True or false questions ask you to write "T" in the answer space if you agree with that statement. If you disagree with the statement, you will circle the incorrect word(s) and write the correct word(s) in the answer space.

Identify the Term That Does Not Belong

In questions that ask you to identify the incorrect term, three words are given that relate to each other in structure or function, and one more word is included that has no relationship or has an opposing relationship to the other three terms. You are asked to circle the term that does not relate to the others. An example might be: iris, cornea, stapes, retina. You would circle the word *stapes* because all other terms refer to the eye.

Fill-in-the-Blank Questions

Fill-in-the-blank questions ask you to recall one or more missing words and insert them into the answer blanks. These questions may involve sentences or paragraphs.

Applying What You Know Questions

Application questions ask you to make judgments about a situation based on the information in the chapter. These questions may concern how you would respond to a situation or ask you to suggest a possible diagnosis for a set of symptoms.

Charts

Several charts have been included that correspond to figures in the text. Areas have been omitted so that you can fill them in and test your recall of these important concepts.

Word Find Puzzles

The Study Guide includes word find puzzles that allow you to identify key terms in the chapter in an interesting and challenging way.

Crossword Puzzles

Vocabulary words from the Language of Science and Language of Medicine sections at the beginning of each chapter of the text have been developed into crossword puzzles. This encourages recall and proper spelling. Each chapter additionally contains an exercise with scrambled words. This also emphasizes recall and proper spelling in a challenging and interesting way.

Labeling Exercises

Labeling exercises present diagrams with parts that are not identified. For each of these diagrams, you are to print the name of each numbered part on the appropriately numbered line. You may choose to further distinguish the structures by coloring them with a variety of colors. After you have written down the names of the structures to be identified, check your answers. When it comes time to review for an examination, you can place a sheet of paper over your answers to test yourself.

After completing the exercises in the Study Guide, check your answers. If they are not correct, refer to the answers page and review it for further clarification. If you still do not understand the question or the answer, ask your instructor for further explanation or assistance.

If you have difficulty with several questions from one section, refer to the pages listed at the end of the section. After reviewing the section, try to answer the questions again. If you are still having difficulty, talk to your instructor.

Check Your Knowledge

This section selects questions from throughout the chapter to provide you with a final review. This mini-test gives you an overview of your knowledge of the entire chapter after completing all of the other sections. It emphasizes the main concepts of the unit but should not be attempted until the specific topics of the chapter have been mastered.

How to Use Visual Memory

Visual memory is another important tool in learning. If I asked you to picture an elephant in your mind, with all its external parts labeled, you could do that easily. Visual memory is a powerful key to learning. Whenever possible, try to build a memory picture. Remember: A picture is worth a thousand words.

Visual memory works especially well with the sequencing of items, such as circulatory pathways and the passage of air or food. Students who try to learn sequencing by memorizing a list of words do poorly on examinations. If they forget one word in the sequence, they then may forget the remaining words as well. With a memory picture you can pick out the important features.

How to Use Mnemonic Devices

Mnemonic devices are little jingles that you memorize to help you remember things. If you make up your own, they will stick with you longer. Here are three examples of such devices:

"On Old Olympus' towering tops a Finn and German viewed some hops." This one is used to remember the cranial nerves. Each word begins with the same letter as does the name of one of the nerves: olfactory, optic, oculomotor, trochlear, trigeminal, abducens, facial, auditory, glossopharyngeal, vagus, sensory (accessory), hypoglossal.

"C. Hopkins CaFe where they serve Mg NaCl." This mnemonic device reminds you of the chemical symbols for the biologically important electrolytes: carbon, hydrogen, oxygen, phosphorus, potassium, iodine, nitrogen, sulfur, calcium, iron, magnesium, sodium, chlorine.

"Roy G. Biv." This mnemonic device helps you remember the colors of the visible light spectrum: red, orange, yellow, green, blue, indigo, violet.

How to Prepare for an Examination

Prepare far in advance for an examination. Actually, your preparation for an examination should begin on the first day of class. Keeping up with your assignments daily makes the final preparation for an examination much easier. You should begin your final preparation at least three nights before the test. Last-minute studying usually means poor results and limited retention.

1. Make sure that you understand and can answer all of the learning objectives for the chapter on which you are being tested.

2. Review the appropriate questions in this Study Guide. Review is something that you should do after every class and at the end of every study session. It is important to keep going over the material until you have a thorough understanding of the chapter and rapid recall of its contents. If review becomes a daily habit, studying for the actual examination will not be difficult. Go through each question and write down an answer. Do the same with the labeling of each structure on the appropriate diagrams.

If you have already done this as part of your daily review, cover the answers with a piece of paper and quiz yourself again.

3. Check the answers that you have written down against the correct answers in the back of the Study Guide. Go back and study the areas in the text that refer to questions that you missed and then try to answer those questions again. If you still cannot answer a question or label a structure correctly, ask your instructor for help.

4. As you read a chapter, ask yourself what questions you would ask if you were writing a test on that unit. You will most likely ask yourself many of the questions that will show up on your examinations.

5. Get a good night's sleep before the test. Staying up late and upsetting your biorhythms will only make you less efficient during the test.

How to Take an Examination

The Day of the Test

1. Get up early enough to avoid rushing. Eat appropriately. Your body needs fuel, but a heavy meal just before a test is not a good idea.

2. Keep calm. Briefly look over your notes. If you have prepared for the test properly, there will be no need for last-minute cramming.

3. Make certain that you have everything you need for the test: pens, pencils, test sheets, and so forth.

4. Allow enough time to get to the examination site. Missing your bus, getting stuck in traffic, or being unable to find a parking space will not put you in a good frame of mind to do well on the examination.

During the Examination

1. Pay careful attention to the instructions for the test.

2. Note any corrections.

3. Budget your time so that you will be able to finish the test.

4. Ask the instructor for clarification if you do not understand a question or an instruction.

5. Concentrate on your own test paper and do not allow yourself to be distracted by others in the room.

Hints for Taking a Multiple Choice Test

1. Read each question carefully. Pay attention to each word.

2. Cross out obviously wrong choices and think about those that are left.

3. Go through the test once, quickly answering the questions you are sure of; then go back over the test and answer the rest of the questions.

4. Fill in the answer spaces completely and make your marks heavy. Erase answers completely if you make a mistake.

5. If you must guess, stick with your first hunch. Most often, students will change right answers to wrong ones.

6. If you will not be penalized for guessing, do not leave any blanks.

Hints for Taking an Essay Test

1. Budget time for each question.

2. Write legibly and try to spell words correctly.

3. Be concise, complete, and specific. Do not be repetitious or long-winded.

4. Organize your answer in an outline—this helps not only you but also the person who grades the test.

5. Answer each question as thoroughly as you can, but leave some room for possible additions.

Hints for Taking a Laboratory Practical Examination

Students often have a hard time with this kind of test. Visual memory is very important here. To put it simply, you must be able to identify every structure you have studied. If you are unable to identify a structure, then you will be unable to answer any questions about that structure.

Questions that could appear on an examination of this type might include:

1. Identification of a structure, organ, or feature
2. Identification of the function of a structure, organ, or feature
3. Sequence questions for air flow, passage of food or urine, and so forth
4. Disease questions (for example, if an organ fails, what disease will result?)

How to Find Out Why Questions Were Missed on an Examination

After the examination, go over your test after it has been scored to see what you missed and why you missed it. You can pick up important clues that will help you on future examinations. Ask yourself these questions:

1. Did I miss questions because I did not read them carefully?
2. Did I miss questions because I had gaps in my knowledge?
3. Did I miss questions because I could not determine scientific words?
4. Did I miss questions because I did not have good visual memory of things?

Be sure to go back and learn the things you did not know. Chances are these topics will come up on the final examination.

Your grades in other classes will improve as well when you apply these study methods. Learning should be fun. With these helpful hints and this Study Guide you should be able to achieve the grades you desire. Good luck!

Contents

UNSCRAMBLE THE WORDS

58. **L X A A I**

59. **Y Y G P H I O O S L**

60. **N O R L A T F**

61. **A S R O D L**

Take the circled letters, unscramble them, and fill in the solution.

What was Becky's favorite music?

62.

APPLYING WHAT YOU KNOW

63. Mrs. Hunt has had an appendectomy. The nurse is preparing to change the dressing. She knows that the appendix is located in the right iliac inguinal region, the distal portion extending at an angle into the hypogastric region. Place an X on the diagram where the nurse will place the dressing.

64. Mrs. Wiedeke noticed a lump in her breast. Dr. Reeder noted on her chart that a small mass was located in the left breast medial to the nipple. Place an X where Mrs. Wiedeke's lump would be located.

65. Heather was injured in a bicycle accident. X-ray films revealed that she had a fracture of the right patella. A cast was applied beginning at the distal femoral region and extending to the pedal region. Place one X where Heather's cast begins and another where it ends.

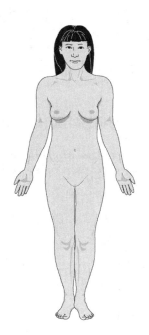

66. Word Find

Find and circle 18 terms presented in this chapter. Words may be spelled top to bottom, bottom to top, right to left, left to right, or diagonally.

Anatomy	Posterior
Atrophy	Proximal
Homeostasis	Sagittal
Medial	Superficial
Mediastinum	Superior
Organ	System
Organization	Thoracic
Physiology	Tissue
Pleural	Ventral

```
N  H  L  T  E  B  W  N  G  N  M  M  Y  X  A
O  O  H  A  V  U  U  C  L  W  E  P  N  G  L
I  M  U  N  I  T  S  A  I  D  E  M  W  A  L
T  E  R  T  V  C  T  S  I  C  J  S  R  T  K
A  O  N  O  P  T  I  A  I  W  A  T  Y  R  H
Z  S  Q  S  I  R  L  F  A  T  N  R  G  O  W
I  T  W  G  P  R  O  I  R  E  T  S  O  P  F
N  A  A  Z  J  E  E  X  V  E  E  H  L  H  Z
A  S  N  L  M  C  T  P  I  C  P  D  O  Y  T
G  I  C  A  Y  U  O  X  U  M  N  U  I  V  P
R  S  M  R  T  N  U  K  B  S  A  Y  S  V  M
O  R  C  U  R  O  I  R  B  S  Q  L  Y  U  G
L  H  X  E  M  P  M  E  T  S  Y  S  H  V  S
U  W  L  L  Q  D  U  Y  Y  N  E  E  P  J  B
Q  N  Z  P  K  D  B  O  D  C  G  I  N  J  A
```

DID YOU KNOW?

- Many animals produce tears, but only humans weep as a result of emotional stress.
- There is speculation that because we no longer have to run for our dinner, and we wear sneakers, the pinkie toe's evolutionary purpose is disappearing and may eventually go away.

KNOW YOUR MEDICAL TERMS

Using the prefixes, root words, and suffixes below, develop new medical terms from this chapter. Words may be used more than once.

Prefixes	Root	Suffixes
hypo	ped	ic
super	stasis	(i)or
dia	ventr	al
homeo	thesis	phragm
epi	later	
ante	gastric	
	brachial	

67. under or below; placing or proposition   _____

68. upon; stomach; relating to   _____

69. front; arm   _____

70. same or equal; standing still _____

71. side; relating to _____

72. foot; relating to _____

73. over or about; quality _____

74. across; enclose _____

75. belly; relating to _____

▶ *If you had difficulty with this section, review pages 4-6.*

CHECK YOUR KNOWLEDGE

Multiple Choice

Circle the correct answer.

1. The body's ability to respond continuously to changes in the environment and maintain consistency in the internal environment is called:
   A. Homeostasis
   B. Superficial
   C. Structural levels
   D. None of the above

2. The regions frequently used by health professionals to locate pain or tumors divide the abdomen into four basic areas called:
   A. Planes
   B. Cavities
   C. Pleural
   D. Quadrants

3. Which of the following organs or structures does *not* lie within the mediastinum?
   A. Thymus
   B. Liver
   C. Esophagus
   D. Trachea

4. A lengthwise plane running from front to back that divides the body into right and left sides is called:
   A. Transverse
   B. Coronal
   C. Frontal
   D. Sagittal

5. A study of the functions of living organisms and their parts is called:
   A. Physiology
   B. Chemistry
   C. Biology
   D. None of the above

6. The thoracic portion of the ventral body cavity is separated from the abdominopelvic portion by a muscle called the:
   A. Latissimus dorsi
   B. Rectus femoris
   C. Diaphragm
   D. Pectoralis

7. An organization of varying numbers and kinds of organs arranged together to perform a complex function is called a:
   A. Cell
   B. Tissue
   C. System
   D. Region

8. The plane that divides superior from inferior is known as the _____ plane.
   A. Transverse
   B. Sagittal
   C. Frontal
   D. None of the above

9. Which of the following structures does *not* lie within the abdominal cavity?
   A. Spleen
   B. Most of the small intestine
   C. Urinary bladder
   D. Stomach

10. Which of the following is an example of an upper abdominal region?
    A. Right iliac region
    B. Left hypochondriac region
    C. Left lumbar region
    D. Hypogastric region

11. The dorsal body cavity contains components of the:
    A. Reproductive system
    B. Digestive system
    C. Respiratory system
    D. Nervous system

12. Which of the following organs is *not* found in the pelvic cavity?
    A. Bladder
    B. Stomach
    C. Rectum
    D. Colon

13. Similar cells acting together to perform a common function exist at a level of organization called a/an:
    A. Organ
    B. Chemical
    C. Tissue
    D. System

14. Which of the following planes would be considered coronal?
    A. A plane that divides the body into anterior and posterior portions
    B. A plane that divides the body into upper and lower portions
    C. A plane that divides the body into right and left sides
    D. A plane that divides the body into superficial and deep portions

15. If your reference point is "nearest to the trunk of the body" versus "farthest from the trunk of the body," where does the elbow lie in relation to the wrist?
    A. Anterior
    B. Posterior
    C. Distal
    D. Proximal

16. In the anatomical position:
    A. The dorsal body cavity is anterior to the ventral
    B. Palms face toward the back of the body
    C. The body is erect
    D. All of the above

17. The buttocks are often used as intramuscular injection sites. This region can be called:
    A. Sacral
    B. Buccal
    C. Cutaneous
    D. Gluteal

18. In the human body, the chest region:
    A. Can be referred to as the thoracic cavity
    B. Is a component of the ventral body cavity
    C. Contains the mediastinum
    D. All of the above

19. Which of the following is *not* a component of the axial subdivision of the body?
    A. Upper extremity
    B. Neck
    C. Trunk
    D. Head

20. The scientific study of disease is:
    A. Dissection
    B. Volar
    C. Pathology
    D. Pathogens

Matching

Match each term in column A with the most appropriate term in column B. Write the corresponding letter in the answer blank. (Only one answer is correct for each.)

Column A

_____ 21. Ventral
_____ 22. Skin
_____ 23. Transverse
_____ 24. Anatomy
_____ 25. Superficial
_____ 26. Pleural
_____ 27. Appendicular
_____ 28. Posterior
_____ 29. Midsagittal
_____ 30. System

Column B

A. Equal
B. Cutaneous
C. Lung
D. Extremities
E. Respiratory
F. Anterior
G. Structure
H. Surface
I. Back
J. Horizontal

DORSAL AND VENTRAL BODY CAVITIES

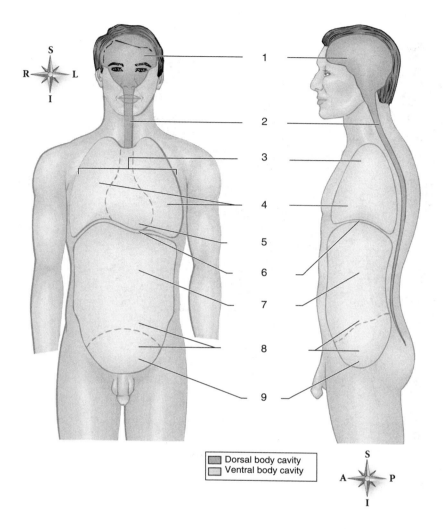

Dorsal body cavity
Ventral body cavity

1. _____   6. _____

2. _____   7. _____

3. _____   8. _____

4. _____   9. _____

5. _____

DIRECTIONS AND PLANES OF THE BODY

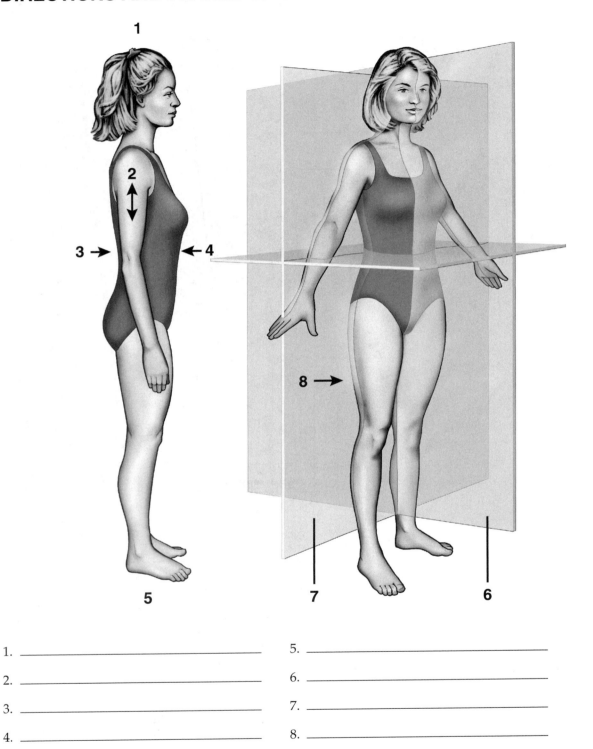

1. _____   5. _____

2. _____   6. _____

3. _____   7. _____

4. _____   8. _____

REGIONS OF THE ABDOMEN

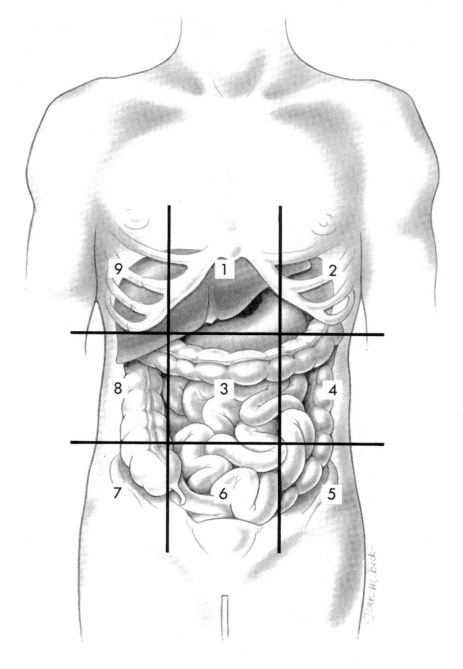

1. _____

2. _____

3. _____

4. _____

5. _____

6. _____

7. _____

8. _____

9. _____

CHAPTER 2

Chemistry of Life

A lthough anatomy can be studied without knowledge of the principles of chemistry, it is hard to imagine having an understanding of physiology without a basic comprehension of chemical reactions in the body. Trillions of cells make up the various levels of organization in the body. Our health and survival depend upon the proper chemical maintenance in the cytoplasm of our cells.

Chemists use the terms *elements* or *compounds* to describe all of the substances (matter) in and around us. What distinguishes these two terms is their basic structure. An element cannot be broken down. A compound, on the other hand, is made up of two or more elements and can be broken down into the elements that form it.

Organic and inorganic compounds are equally important to our survival. Without organic compounds, such as carbohydrates, proteins, and fats, and inorganic compounds, such as water, we could not sustain life.

Because we cannot see many of the chemical reactions that take place daily in our bodies, it is sometimes difficult to comprehend the principles involved in initiating them. Chemicals are responsible for directing virtually all of our bodily functions. Therefore, it is important to master the fundamental concepts of chemistry in order to understand physiology.

TOPICS FOR REVIEW

Before progressing to Chapter 3, you should have an understanding of the basic chemical reactions in the body and the fundamental concepts of biochemistry.

LEVELS OF CHEMICAL ORGANIZATION

Multiple Choice

Circle the correct answer.

1. Which of the following is *not* a subatomic particle?
   A. Proton
   B. Electron
   C. Isotope
   D. Neutron

2. Electrons move about within certain limits called:
   A. Energy levels
   B. Orbitals
   C. Chemical bonding
   D. Shells

3. The number of protons in the nucleus is an atom's:
   A. Atomic mass
   B. Atomic energy level
   C. Atomic number
   D. None of the above

4. The number of protons and neutrons combined is the atom's:
   A. Atomic mass
   B. Atomic energy level
   C. Orbit
   D. Chemical bonding

5. Which of the following is *not* one of the major elements present in the human body?
   A. Oxygen
   B. Carbon
   C. Nitrogen
   D. Iron

6. Atoms usually unite with each other to form larger chemical units called:
   A. Energy levels
   B. Mass
   C. Molecules
   D. Shells

7. Substances whose molecules have more than one element in them are called:
   A. Compounds
   B. Orbitals
   C. Elements
   D. Neutrons

True or False

For each of the following statements, write "T" in the answer blank if it is true. If the statement is false, circle the incorrect word(s) and write the correct word(s) in the answer blank.

_____ 8. *Matter* is anything that occupies space and has mass.

_____ 9. In the body, most chemicals are in the form of electrons.

_____ 10. At the core of each atom is a nucleus composed of positively charged protons and negatively charged neutrons.

_____ 11. Orbitals are arranged into *energy levels* depending on their distance from the nucleus.

_____ 12. The *formula* for a compound contains symbols that represent each element in the molecule.

▷ *If you had difficulty with this section, review pages 24-29.*

CHEMICAL BONDING

Multiple Choice

Circle the correct answer.

13. Ionic bonds are chemical bonds formed by the:
    A. Sharing of electrons between atoms
    B. Donation of protons from one atom to another
    C. Donation of electrons from one atom to another
    D. Acceptance of protons from one atom to another

14. Molecules that form ions when dissolved in water are called:
    A. Covalent bonds
    B. Electrolytes
    C. Isotopes
    D. Ionic bonds

15. When atoms share electrons, a/an _____ forms.
    A. Covalent bond
    B. Electrolyte
    C. Ionic bond
    D. Isotope

16. Covalent bonds:
    A. Break apart easily in water
    B. Are not easily broken
    C. Donate electrons
    D. None of the above

17. An example of an ionic bond is:
    A. NaCl
    B. Ca
    C. O
    D. P

18. If a molecule "dissociates" in water, it:
    A. Has taken on additional ions
    B. Has eliminated ions
    C. Separates to form free ions
    D. Forms a covalent bond

▷ *If you had difficulty with this section, review pages 29-30.*

INORGANIC CHEMISTRY

Match each term with its corresponding description or definition.

_____ 19. A type of compound
_____ 20. Compound essential to life
_____ 21. Dissolves solutes
_____ 22. Water plus common salt
_____ 23. Reactants combine only after (H) and (O) atoms are removed
_____ 24. Combine to form a larger product
_____ 25. The reverse of dehydration synthesis
_____ 26. Yields energy for muscle contraction
_____ 27. Alkaline compound
_____ 28. A measure of the H^+ concentration
_____ 29. Easily dissociates to form H^+ ions
_____ 30. Dissociates very little

A. Aqueous solution
B. Water
C. ATP
D. Base
E. Solvent
F. pH
G. Dehydration synthesis
H. Inorganic
I. Weak acid
J. Hydrolysis
K. Strong acid
L. Reactants

▷ *If you had difficulty with this section, review pages 30-33.*

ORGANIC CHEMISTRY

Match each numbered term with its category. Write the corresponding letter in the blank.

A. Carbohydrate   B. Lipid   C. Protein   D. Nucleic acid

_____ 31. Monosaccharide

_____ 32. Triglyceride

_____ 33. DNA

_____ 34. Cholesterol

_____ 35. Amino acid

_____ 36. Glycogen

_____ 37. Sucrose

_____ 38. Phospholipid

_____ 39. Contains C, O, H, and N

_____ 40. RNA

▷ *If you had difficulty with this section, review pages 33-38.*

UNSCRAMBLE THE WORDS

41. **N T E I P O R**

☐☐☐◯☐☐☐

42. **S E B A**

☐☐◯☐

43. **K L A L A N I E**

☐☐☐☐◯☐☐☐☐

44. **D L P I I**

◯☐☐☐☐

Take the circled letters, unscramble them, and fill in the solution.

What was missing from the Thanksgiving dinner?

45. ☐☐☐☐☐

CHEMISTRY OF LIFE

Fill in the crossword puzzle.

ACROSS

1. Below 7.0 on pH scale
2. Bond formed by sharing electrons
5. Occupies space and has mass
6. Reverse of dehydration synthesis
7. Substances composed of one type of atom
8. Uncharged subatomic particle
9. Subatomic particle

DOWN

1. Combine to form molecules
2. Substances whose molecules have more than one element
3. Amino acid
4. Polysaccharide
7. Chemical catalyst
10. Fat

KNOW YOUR MEDICAL TERMS

Select the correct term for the given literal definitions below.

46. _____ apart; unite; action
47. _____ cushion; actor
48. _____ many; sugar; chemical
49. _____ bile; solid; oil
50. _____ band
51. _____ not; natural; to assemble
52. _____ water; produce

a. buffer
b. hydrogen
c. cholesterol
d. dissociate
e. polysaccharide
f. inorganic compound
g. bond

▷ *If you had difficulty with this section, review pages 26 and 27.*

APPLYING WHAT YOU KNOW

53. Kim just finished preparing a meal of pan-fried hamburgers for her family. While the frying pan was still hot, she poured the liquid grease into a metal container to cool. Later, she noticed that the liquid oil had solidified as it cooled. Explain the chemistry of why the then room-temperature fat was solid.

54. Carol was gaining weight, yet she was eating very little. Her physician suspected hypothyroidism and suggested a test that measures radiation emitted by the thyroid when radioactive iodine is introduced into the gland. Describe what the radiologist will do to evaluate Carol's thyroid function.

55.   Word Find

Find and circle 12 terms presented in this chapter. Words may be spelled top to bottom, bottom to top, right to left, left to right, or diagonally.

Alkaline
Atomic mass
Base
Carbohydrate
Dehydration
Dissociation

Electrolyte
Molecule
Nucleic acid
Proton
Reactant
Solvent

```
E T A R D Y H O B R A C E
T B H S I H L I N A T O D
B N E H S G O U L P O T E
R Z A M S F R K U S M T H
P R O T O N A I E C I X Y
B R N U C L E I C A C I D
C A F T I A E W G G M W R
L E S N A B E C E E A E A
G Q E E T E A R U S S F T
Q R P V I B Y K I L S W I
E T Y L O R T C E L E B O
S B U O N E S P N B R B N
O P J S T D J M O L U H D
```

DID YOU KNOW?

• After a vigorous workout, your triglycerides fall 10% to 20%, and your HDL increases by the same percentage for 2 to 3 hours.

• Being right-handed can prolong your life. Right-handed people live 5 to 9 years longer than left-handed people.

CHECK YOUR KNOWLEDGE

Fill in the blanks.

1. _____ is the field of science devoted to studying the chemical aspects of life.

2. Atoms are composed of protons, electrons, and _____.

3. The farther an orbital extends from the nucleus, the _____ its energy level.

4. Substances can be classified as _____ or

   _____.

5. Chemical bonds form to make atoms more _____.

6. A(n) _____ is an electrically charged atom.

7. Few _____ compounds have carbon atoms in them and none have C—C or C—H bonds.

8. _____ _____ is a reaction in which water is lost from the reactants.

9. Chemists often use a _____ _____ to represent a chemical reaction.

10. High levels of _____ in the blood make the blood more acidic.

11. _____ are compounds that produce an excess of H^+ ions.

12. _____ maintain pH balance by preventing sudden changes in the H^+ ion concentration.

13. _____ literally means "carbon" and "water."

14. _____ is a steroid lipid.

15. Collagen and keratin are examples of _____ proteins.

16. A _____ _____

    _____ is formed when the twists and folds of the secondary structure fold again to form a three-dimensional structure.

17. A _____ _____

    _____ is a sequence of amino acids in a chain.

18. In the DNA molecule, nucleotides are arranged in a twisted strand called a

    _____ _____.

19. RNA uses the same set of bases as DNA except for the substitution of

    _____ for thymine.

20. Glycogen and starch are examples of _____.

CHAPTER 3

Cells

Cells are the smallest structural units of living things. Therefore, because we are living, we are made up of a mass of cells. Human cells, which vary in shape and size, can be seen only under a microscope. The three main parts of a cell are the cytoplasmic membrane, the cytoplasm, and the nucleus. As you review this chapter, you will be amazed at the correlation between a cell and the body as a whole. You will identify miniature circulatory systems, reproductive systems, digestive systems, power plants (much like muscular systems), and many other structures that will aid in your understanding of these body systems in future chapters.

Cells—just like humans—require water, food, gases, the elimination of wastes, and numerous other substances and processes in order to survive. The movement of these substances into and out of cells is accomplished by two primary methods: passive transport processes and active transport processes. In passive transport processes, no cellular energy is required to effect movement through the cell membrane. However, in active transport processes, cellular energy is required to provide movement through the cell membrane.

The study of cell reproduction completes this chapter's overview of cells. A basic explanation of DNA, "the hereditary molecule," illuminates the due respect for the amazing capability of the cell to transmit physical and mental traits from generation to generation. Reproduction of the cell—mitosis—is a complex process made up of several stages. These stages are outlined and diagrammed in the text to facilitate learning.

This chapter concludes with a discussion of changes that may occur during cell growth and reproduction. Knowledge of the structure, characteristics, and function of cells is necessary to continue your understanding of the levels of organization in the body.

TOPICS FOR REVIEW

Before progressing to Chapter 4, you should have an understanding of the structure and function of the smallest living unit in the body—the cell. Your review should also include the methods by which substances move through the cell membrane and the stages that occur during cell reproduction. As you finish this chapter, you should have an understanding of tonicity and how the concentration of body fluids impacts cellular health.

CELLS

Match each term on the left with its corresponding description on the right.

Group A

1. Cytoplasm	A. Component of plasma membrane
2. Plasma membrane	B. Controls genetic code of the cell
3. Cholesterol	C. "Living matter"
4. Nucleus	D. Organizes and moves structures within the cell
5. Centrosome	E. Surrounds cells

Group B

6. Ribosomes	A. "Power plants"
7. Endoplasmic reticulum	B. "Digestive bags"
8. Mitochondria	C. "Chemical processing and packaging center"
9. Lysosomes	D. "Protein factories"
10. Golgi apparatus	E. "Smooth and rough"

Fill in the blanks.

11. The fat molecule _____ helps stabilize the phospholipid molecules to prevent breakage of the plasma membrane.

12. A procedure performed before transplanting an organ from one individual to another is

_____ _____.

13. Fine, hairlike extensions found on the exposed or free surfaces of some cells are called

_____.

14. Which organelle is distinguished by the fact that it has two types; it can be either smooth or rough.

_____ _____.

15. _____ are usually attached to the rough endoplasmic reticulum and produce enzymes and other protein compounds.

16. The _____ provide energy-releasing chemical reactions that go on continuously.

17. The organelles that can digest and destroy microbes that invade the cell are called

_____.

18. Mucus is an example of a product manufactured by the _____

_____.

19. Rod-shaped structures, known as _____, play an important role during cell division.

20. _____ _____ are threadlike structures made up of proteins and DNA.

21. Movement of the _____ of a sperm cell is an example of a specialized organelle having a specialized function.

22. _____ increase the absorption rate of nutrients in the blood.

▷ *If you had difficulty with this section, review pages 42-52.*

MOVEMENT OF SUBSTANCES THROUGH CELL MEMBRANES

Circle the correct answer.

23. The energy required for active transport processes is obtained from:
    A. ATP
    B. DNA
    C. Diffusion
    D. Osmosis

24. An example of a passive transport process is:
    A. Permease system
    B. Phagocytosis
    C. Pinocytosis
    D. Diffusion

25. Movement of substances from a region of high concentration to a region of low concentration is known as:
    A. Active transport
    B. Passive transport
    C. Cellular energy
    D. Concentration gradient

26. Osmosis is the _____ of water across a selectively permeable membrane.
    A. Filtration
    B. Equilibrium
    C. Active transport
    D. Diffusion

27. _____ involves the movement of solutes across a selectively permeable membrane by the process of diffusion.
    A. Osmosis
    B. Filtration
    C. Dialysis
    D. Phagocytosis

28. A specialized example of diffusion is:
    A. Osmosis
    B. Permease system
    C. Filtration
    D. All of the above

29. Which movement always occurs down a hydrostatic pressure gradient?
    A. Osmosis
    B. Filtration
    C. Dialysis
    D. Facilitated diffusion

30. The uphill movement of a substance through a living cell membrane is:
    A. Osmosis
    B. Diffusion
    C. Active transport process
    D. Passive transport process

31. The ion pump is an example of what type of movement?
    A. Gravity
    B. Hydrostatic pressure
    C. Active transport process
    D. Passive transport process

32. An example of a cell capable of phagocytosis is the:
    A. White blood cell
    B. Red blood cell
    C. Muscle cell
    D. Bone cell

33. A salt solution that contains a higher concentration of salt than living red blood cells would be:
    A. Hypotonic
    B. Hypertonic
    C. Isotonic
    D. Homeostatic

34. A red blood cell becomes engorged with water and will eventually lyse, releasing hemoglobin into the solution. This solution is _____ to the red blood cell.
    A. Hypotonic
    B. Hypertonic
    C. Isotonic
    D. Homeostatic

▷ *If you had difficulty with this section, review pages 52-57.*

CELL REPRODUCTION AND HEREDITY

Circle the word in each word group that does not belong.

35. DNA	Adenine	Uracil	Thymine
36. Complementary base pairing	Guanine	RNA	Cytosine
37. Anaphase	Specific sequence	Gene	Base pairs
38. RNA	Ribose	Thymine	Uracil
39. Translation	Protein synthesis	mRNA	Interphase
40. Cleavage furrow	Anaphase	Prophase	2 daughter cells
41. Preparatory stage	Prophase	Interphase	DNA replication
42. Identical	Two nuclei	Telophase	Metaphase
43. Metaphase	Prophase	Telophase	Gene

▷ *If you had difficulty with this section, review pages 57-63.*

UNSCRAMBLE THE WORDS

44. **T H I R A E E N P S**

45. **E R I L C T E O N**

46. **U I I F O N S D F**

47. **O E E P A T S H L**

48. **R A N L G L E E O**

Take the circled letters, unscramble them, and fill in the solution.

Why Susie asked Carlos to read a letter from her friend Juan.

49.

APPLYING WHAT YOU KNOW

50. Mr. Fee's boat capsized, and consequently he was stranded on a deserted shoreline for 2 days without food or water. When found, he had swallowed a great deal of seawater. He was taken to the emergency room in a state of dehydration. In the space below, draw the appearance of Mr. Fee's red blood cells as they would appear to the laboratory technician.

51. The nurse was instructed to dissolve a pill in a small amount of liquid medication. Just as she dropped the capsule into the liquid, she was interrupted by the telephone. On her return to the medication cart, she found the medication completely dissolved and apparently scattered evenly throughout the liquid. This phenomenon did not surprise her because she was aware from her knowledge of cell transport

    that _____ had created this distribution.

52. Ms. Bence has emphysema and has been admitted to the hospital unit with oxygen administered per nasal cannula. Emphysema destroys the tiny air sacs in the lungs. These tiny air sacs, alveoli, provide what function for Ms. Bence?

53. Word Find

Find and circle 16 terms presented in this chapter. Words may be spelled top to bottom, bottom to top, right to left, left to right, or diagonally.

```
A  P  D  I  E  V  E  W  N  P  F  E  H  Y  X
I  G  I  Z  N  S  R  L  X  S  T  W  F  Z  S
R  J  V  N  N  T  A  I  L  M  R  P  H  M  F
D  W  U  E  O  O  E  H  B  E  A  D  U  G  F
N  W  I  U  I  C  I  R  P  O  N  N  F  B  W
O  P  U  R  S  H  Y  T  P  O  S  A  W  X  K
H  X  F  O  U  R  Y  T  A  H  L  O  G  A  W
C  L  Z  N  F  O  Y  P  O  R  A  E  M  R  M
O  U  I  X  F  M  L  F  O  S  T  S  T  E  O
T  T  B  Y  I  A  B  C  O  T  I  L  E  S  D
I  V  S  O  D  T  T  M  I  T  O  S  I  S  U
M  N  A  A  I  I  L  E  N  L  N  N  N  F  R
E  O  K  K  I  D  C  Q  H  B  I  V  I  T  H
E  K  T  X  B  Z  A  E  A  L  S  A  E  C  K
S  B  Z  R  P  M  V  L  X  W  Z  A  Z  C  V
```

Chromatid	Hypotonic	Pinocytosis
Cilia	Interphase	Ribosome
Cuboidal	Mitochondria	Telophase
DNA	Mitosis	Translation
Diffusion	Neuron	
Filtration	Organelle	

KNOW YOUR MEDICAL TERMS

Match the term on the left with the literal translation on the right.

54. _____ Hyperplasia   A. Scalloped process
55. _____ Flagellum   B. Produce entire collection
56. _____ Atrophy   C. Drink cell condition
57. _____ Pinocytosis   D. Apart loosening
58. _____ Crenation   E. Push condition
59. _____ Osmosis   F. Excessive shape
60. _____ Genome   G. Whip
61. _____ Dialysis   H. Without nourishment state

▷ *If you had difficulty with this section, review pages 44-45.*

DID YOU KNOW?

• The largest single cell in the human body is the female sex cell, the ovum. The smallest single cell in the human body is the male sex cell, the sperm.
• The smarter you are, the more you dream. Some people even think they are smarter in their dreams than when they are awake!

CELLS

Fill in the crossword puzzle.

ACROSS

1. Shriveling of cell due to water withdrawal
8. Energy source for active transport
9. Reproduction process of most cells
10. Cell organ
11. Cartilage cell
12. First stage of mitosis
13. Occurs when substances scatter themselves evenly throughout an available space

DOWN

2. Ribonucleic acid (abbreviation)
3. Last stage of mitosis
4. Nerve cell
5. Literally means "center part"
6. Specialized example of diffusion
7. Having an osmotic pressure greater than that of the solution

CHECK YOUR KNOWLEDGE

Multiple Choice

Circle the correct answer.

1. Which of the following cellular structures has the ability to secrete digestive enzymes?
   A. Lysosomes
   B. Mitochondria
   C. Golgi apparatus
   D. Ribosomes

2. Red blood cells do what when placed in a hypertonic salt solution?
   A. Remain unchanged
   B. Undergo crenation
   C. Lyse
   D. None of the above

3. Which of the following statements is true of chromatin granules?
   A. They exist in the cell cytoplasm.
   B. They are made up of DNA.
   C. They form spindle fibers.
   D. All of the above

4. In which stage of mitosis do chromosomes move to opposite ends of the cell along the spindle fibers?
   A. Anaphase
   B. Metaphase
   C. Prophase
   D. Telophase

5. Filtration is a process that involves which of the following?
   A. Active transport
   B. The expenditure of energy
   C. Changes in hydrostatic pressure
   D. All of the above

6. The synthesis of proteins by ribosomes using information coded in the mRNA molecule is called what?
   A. Translation
   B. Transcription
   C. Replication
   D. Crenation

7. The genetic code for a particular protein is passed from DNA to mRNA by a process known as:
   A. Transcription
   B. Translation
   C. Interphase
   D. Genome

8. If a strand of DNA has a base sequence of AGGC, the complementary pair for that strand will be:
   A. TCCG
   B. CCTG
   C. TTCG
   D. TUUG

9. Which of the following is not true of RNA?
   A. It is a single strand.
   B. It contains uracil rather than thymine.
   C. The base pairs are adenine and uracil and guanine and cytosine.
   D. It contains deoxyribose sugar.

10. All of the DNA in each cell of the body is called the:
    A. Tissue typing
    B. Genome
    C. Gene
    D. Genetic code

Matching

Match each term in column A with the most appropriate term in column B. (Only one answer is correct for each.)

Column A

11. _____ Dialysis
12. _____ Plasma membrane
13. _____ Isotonic
14. _____ Pinocytosis
15. _____ Prophase
16. _____ Adenine
17. _____ Diffusion
18. _____ Hypertonic solution
19. _____ Mitochondria
20. _____ Ion pump

Column B

A. Chromatids
B. Thymine
C. Active transport
D. Energy
E. Carrier protein
F. Diffusion
G. Phospholipids
H. Crenation
I. Passive transport
J. Blood cells

CELL STRUCTURE

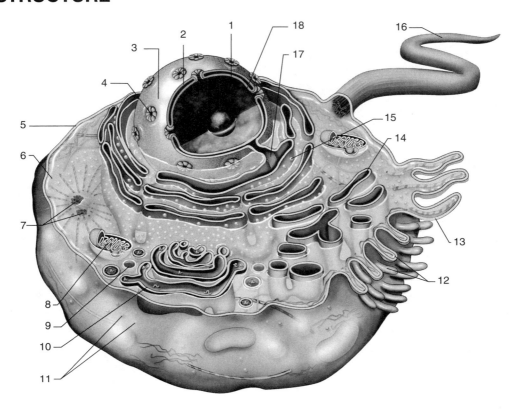

1. _____
2. _____
3. _____
4. _____
5. _____
6. _____
7. _____
8. _____
9. _____

10. _____
11. _____
12. _____
13. _____
14. _____
15. _____
16. _____
17. _____
18. _____

MITOSIS

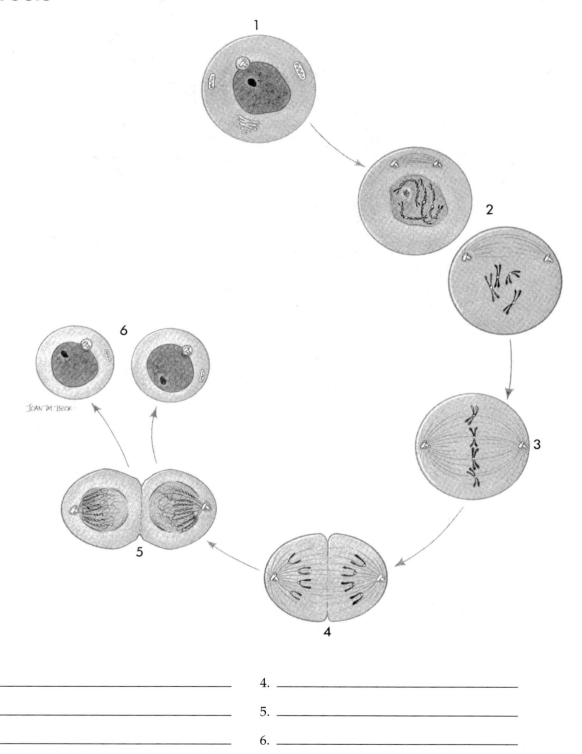

1. _____

2. _____

3. _____

4. _____

5. _____

6. _____

CHAPTER 4

Tissues

After successfully completing the study of the cell, you are ready to progress to the next level of anatomical structure: tissues. Four principal types of tissue, epithelial, connective, muscle, and nervous, perform multiple functions to ensure that homeostasis is maintained. Among these functions are protection, absorption, excretion, support, insulation, conduction of impulses, movement of bones, and destruction of bacteria. This variety of functions gives us a real appreciation for the complexity of this level. A macroscopic view confirms this statement as we marvel at the fact that soft, sticky, liquid blood and sturdy compact bone are both considered tissues. As you view the various tissue slides in your text and under a microscope, you will observe the various shapes, arrangement of cells, and general characteristics of each unique type. These numerous distinctions also help explain the varying ability of tissues to regenerate or repair after trauma, disease, or injury.

The chapter concludes with a discussion of changes that may occur during cell growth and reproduction. Knowledge of the characteristics and functions of tissues is necessary to complete your understanding of this structural level of organization and to successfully bridge your knowledge between the cell and the study of body organs.

TOPICS FOR REVIEW

Before progressing to Chapter 5, you should thoroughly review the types of tissues and the unique characteristics of each one. You should also have a basic understanding of how tissue repair is accomplished and the possible effect of that repair on the body.

INTRODUCTION TO TISSUES

Multiple Choice

Circle the correct answer.

1. A tissue is:
   A. A membrane that lines body cavities
   B. A group of similar cells that perform a unique function to help the organ do its job
   C. A thin sheet of cells embedded in a matrix
   D. The most complex organizational unit of the body

2. The four principal types of tissues include all of the following *except*:
   A. Nervous
   B. Muscle
   C. Cartilage
   D. Connective

3. Tissues differ from each other in the:
   A. Size and shape of their cells
   B. Amount and kind of material between the cells
   C. Special functions they perform
   D. All of the above

   ▷ *If you had difficulty with this section, review pages 70-73.*

EPITHELIAL TISSUE

Circle the correct answer.

4. Which of the following is *not* a function of epithelium?
   A. Secretion
   B. Protection
   C. Absorption
   D. All of the above are functions of the membranous epithelium.

5. Which of the following is *not* a structural example of epithelium?
   A. Stratified squamous
   B. Simple transitional
   C. Simple columnar
   D. Pseudostratified

6. Epithelial cells can be classified according to shape. Which of the following is not a characteristic shape of epithelium?
   A. Cuboidal
   B. Rectangular
   C. Squamous
   D. Columnar

7. Endocrine glands discharge their products into:
   A. Body cavities
   B. Blood
   C. Organ surfaces
   D. None of the above

8. Which statement regarding pseudostratified epithelium is false?
   A. Basement membrane lies beneath pseudostratified epithelium.
   B. *Pseudo* means "false."
   C. Pseudostratified epithelium is two layers thick.
   D. Pseudostratified epithelium lines the trachea.

Matching

Match the arrangement of epithelial cells with its corresponding description.

9. _____ Single layer of cube-shaped cells

10. _____ Multiple layers of cells with flat cells at the outer surface

11. _____ Single layer of flat, scalelike cells

12. _____ Single layer of tall, thin cells that compose the surface of mucous membranes

13. _____ Cilia from this tissue move mucus along the lining surface of the trachea

14. _____ Typically found in body areas subjected to stress and must be able to stretch

A. Simple squamous
B. Simple cuboidal
C. Simple columnar
D. Pseudostratified
E. Stratified squamous
F. Stratified transitional

Tissue Labeling

Label the following images and identify the principal tissue type of each. Be as specific as possible. Consult your textbook if you need assistance.

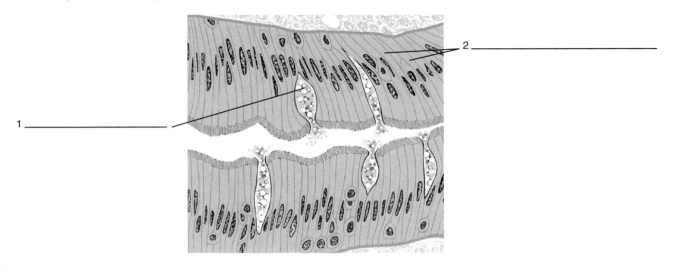

1. Tissue type: _____

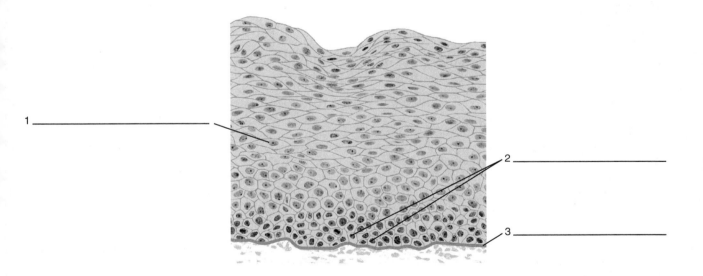

2. Tissue type: _____

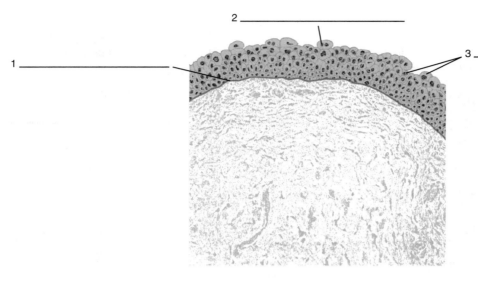

2 _____

3 _____

1 _____

3. Tissue type: _____

 If you had difficulty with this section, review pages 70-77.

CONNECTIVE TISSUE

Multiple Choice

Circle the correct answer.

15. Which of the following is *not* an example of connective tissue?
    A. Transitional
    B. Adipose
    C. Blood
    D. Bone

16. Adipose tissue performs which of the following functions?
    A. Insulation
    B. Protection
    C. Support
    D. All of the above

17. The basic structural unit of bone is the microscopic:
    A. Osteon
    B. Lacunae
    C. Lamellae
    D. Canaliculi

18. The term *osteon* is synonymous with:
    A. Cartilage
    B. Chondrocyte
    C. Haversian system
    D. Osteoblast

19. Dense fibrous connective tissue consists mainly of:
    A. White collagen fibers
    B. Liquid matrix
    C. Goblet cells
    D. Glands

20. Which statement is false regarding connective tissue?
    A. It is the most abundant tissue.
    B. It is widely distributed throughout the body.
    C. It exists in more varied forms than any of the other tissue types.
    D. It is voluntary.

Tissue Labeling

Label the following images and identify the principal tissue type of each.

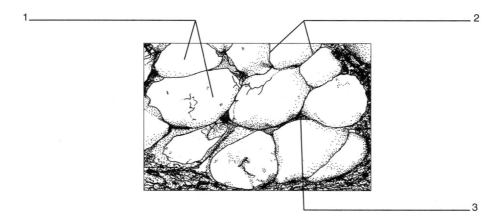

4. Tissue type: _____

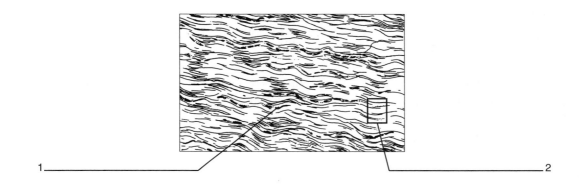

5. Tissue type: _____

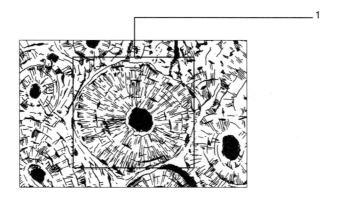

6. Tissue type: _____

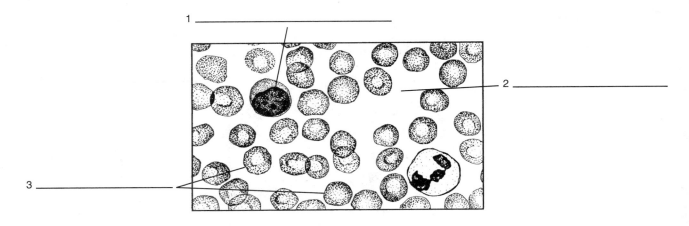

7. Tissue type: _____

▷ *If you had difficulty with this section, review pages 77-80.*

MUSCLE TISSUE

Matching

Identify the type of muscle tissue with its corresponding definition.

21. _____ Cylindrical, striated, voluntary cells
22. _____ Nonstriated, involuntary, narrow fibers with only one nucleus per fiber
23. _____ Striated, branching, involuntary cells with intercalated disks
24. _____ Responsible for willed body movements
25. _____ Also called *visceral muscle*
26. _____ Found in the walls of hollow internal organs

A. Cardiac muscle
B. Skeletal muscle
C. Smooth muscle

Tissue Labeling

Label the following images and identify the principal tissue type of each.

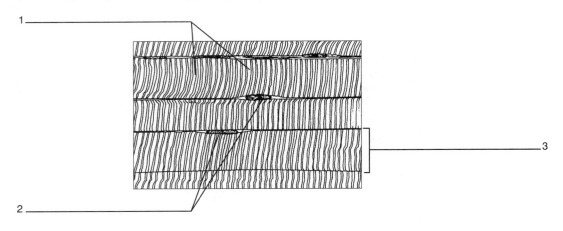

8. Tissue type: _____

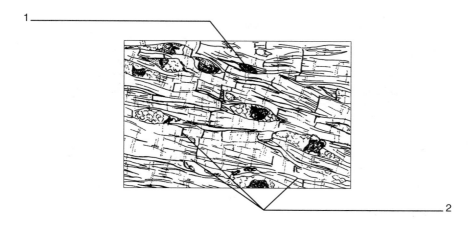

9. Tissue type: _____

▷ *If you had difficulty with this section, review pages 80-82.*

NERVOUS TISSUE

Matching

Match each term with its corresponding description.

27. _____ Supportive cells

28. _____ Cell process that transmits nerve impulses away from the cell body

29. _____ The conducting cells of the nervous system

30. _____ Cell process that carries nerve impulses toward the cell body.

A. Neuron

B. Neuroglia

C. Axon

D. Dendrite

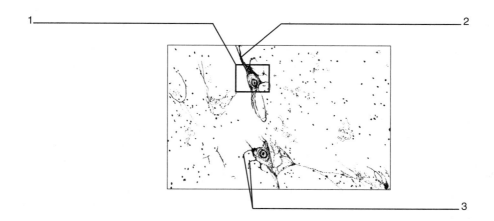

10. Tissue type: _____

▷ *If you had difficulty with this section, review pages 82-83.*

TISSUES

31. Fill in the missing areas of the chart.

TISSUE	LOCATION	FUNCTION
Epithelial		
1. Simple squamous	1a. Alveoli of lungs	1a.
	1b. Lining of blood and lymphatic vessels	1b.
2. Stratified squamous	2a.	2a. Protection
	2b.	2b. Protection
3. Simple columnar	3.	3. Protection, secretion, absorption
4.	4. Urinary bladder	4. Protection
5. Pseudostratified	5.	5. Protection
6. Simple cuboidal	6. Glands; kidney tubules	6.
Connective		
1. Areolar	1.	1. Connection
2.	2. Under skin	2. Protection; insulation
3. Dense fibrous	3. Tendons; ligaments; fascia; scar tissue	3.
4. Bone	4.	4. Support, protection
5. Cartilage	5.	5. Firm but flexible support
6. Blood	6. Blood vessels	6.
7.	7. Red bone marrow	7. Blood cell formation
Muscle		
1. Skeletal (striated voluntary)	1.	1. Movement of bones
2.	2. Wall of heart	2. Contraction of heart
3. Smooth	3.	3. Movement of substances along ducts; change in diameter of pupils and shape of lens; "gooseflesh"
Nervous		
1.	1.	1. Irritability, conduction

▶ *If you had difficulty with this section, review Tables 4-1, 4-2, and 4-3 and pages 73-83.*

TISSUE REPAIR

Fill in the blanks.

32. _____ is the growth of new tissue (as opposed to scarring.)

33. A _____ is an unusually thick scar.

34. Tissues usually repair themselves by allowing _____ cells to remove dead or injured cells.

35. Epithelial and _____ tissues have the greatest capacity to regenerate.

36. Like muscle tissue, _____ tissue has a very limited capacity to regenerate.

UNSCRAMBLE THE WORDS

37. **E D I N E D T R**

38. **E S T O N O**

39. **U M A S S U O Q**

40. **S I F R D A I E T T**

41. **L A I G**

Take the circled letters, unscramble them, and fill in the solution.

What Madison's friend gave her when she tripped and fell.

42.

APPLYING WHAT YOU KNOW

43. Merrily is 5'4" and weighs 115 lbs. She appears very healthy and fit, yet her doctor advised her that she is "overfat." What might be the explanation for this assessment?

44. Holly is a bodybuilder who is obsessed with her physique. She exercises daily and eats a very low-fat diet. A personal fitness trainer has assessed her body fat at 12%. Determine whether she is too lean or too fat. Explain the relationship between her body-fat percentage and lifestyle.

45. Word Find

Find and circle 16 terms presented in this chapter. Words may be spelled top to bottom, bottom to top, right to left, left to right, or diagonally.

```
A  T  K  C  A  O  C  J  A  W  Y  O  F  A  V  A  R  G  I  T  Q  W  A  L
I  D  N  D  N  S  F  D  W  P  G  V  P  U  C  P  D  R  T  X  B  P  N  R
H  Y  P  E  R  P  L  A  S  I  A  V  W  B  Z  L  E  I  O  D  K  S  C  Y
L  V  G  M  K  T  M  B  H  Y  L  S  P  J  O  S  I  Z  P  X  W  F  J  E
I  F  L  V  C  M  A  T  R  I  X  T  K  M  M  W  O  U  U  O  B  O  M  P
P  K  O  F  T  A  U  Z  E  E  H  R  A  J  K  K  Y  Z  I  M  S  V  C  I
U  Q  A  L  B  P  T  U  R  N  W  H  T  F  R  V  Q  C  F  O  D  E  P  T
U  U  H  Q  K  K  E  N  B  X  I  S  E  M  G  M  U  S  C  L  E  Q  F  H
S  P  A  U  P  U  O  W  G  K  S  O  B  M  C  A  F  Q  B  C  A  T  C  E
Y  W  K  J  O  B  J  L  Q  D  B  M  J  M  A  E  Z  N  I  Z  U  A  A  L
M  L  B  I  K  Y  U  T  O  V  E  B  L  H  D  T  Z  S  P  F  U  E  R  I
R  E  G  E  N  E  R  A  T  I  O  N  Q  W  K  Z  O  K  V  C  S  H  T  A
U  U  P  X  V  I  M  A  E  Q  P  Z  O  F  Z  M  W  P  X  W  X  H  I  L
E  V  Y  M  P  U  C  N  P  M  B  P  Q  U  F  R  K  M  O  R  X  I  L  V
T  L  N  Z  I  N  N  Z  I  P  O  X  B  Q  P  T  K  U  L  I  U  G  A  T
I  J  O  B  U  D  C  E  Q  S  E  Y  H  N  S  Y  L  K  N  G  E  U  G  R
O  D  L  E  M  U  S  P  P  X  U  V  O  O  F  M  Z  O  V  S  M  T  E  E
S  C  E  G  M  U  K  X  Y  W  S  X  T  L  A  J  Q  H  E  E  T  G  I  P
M  F  V  V  Z  X  Z  G  K  T  A  Q  J  T  S  O  D  M  Z  M  D  J  T  C
E  T  R  A  N  S  I  T  I  O  N  A  L  R  C  F  Z  F  N  U  A  M  S  O
Q  W  T  C  Y  F  H  H  A  R  L  B  V  F  I  E  J  Y  M  I  D  Z  D  N
G  O  Q  W  N  J  A  N  R  I  W  T  Z  R  A  N  M  U  L  O  C  H  V  N
Q  Q  M  V  L  A  D  I  O  B  U  C  Y  A  S  F  G  D  V  L  U  M  J  E
S  K  T  C  H  P  Q  I  X  D  Y  O  V  K  L  T  M  E  I  A  S  Z  O  C
X  D  D  R  N  W  T  W  O  K  H  N  P  F  D  M  P  P  H  O  E  T  H  T
N  K  P  S  E  U  D  O  S  T  R  A  T  I  F  I  E  D  G  L  L  C  K  I
I  V  M  X  A  P  L  T  E  S  W  Z  B  U  W  Z  I  I  W  W  F  E  C  V
J  Q  X  T  L  J  M  O  B  D  G  F  V  E  H  Z  Y  F  Y  I  N  W  K  E
```

Adipose	Connective	Hematopoietic	Muscle
Axon	Cuboidal	Hyperplasia	Pseudostratified
Cartilage	Epithelial	Keloid	Regeneration
Columnar	Fascia	Matrix	Transitional

DID YOU KNOW?

- As many as 500,000 Americans die from cancer each year. That's more than all the lives lost in the past 100 years by the U.S. military forces. Half of all cancers are diagnosed in people under the age of 67.
- Your smell or body odor is unique to you unless you have a twin. Even babies recognize the scent of their mother.

KNOW YOUR MEDICAL TERMS

Fill in the missing medical word or word parts.

46. anti _____ gen _____

47. axle _____

48. cartilag _____

49. glue _____ produce _____

50. endo _____ crin _____

51. osteo _____ on _____

52. acorn _____

53. kel _____ oid _____

54. layer _____ made _____

55. scale _____ characterized by _____

▶ *If you had difficulty with this section, review pages 72 and 73.*

TISSUES

Fill in the crossword puzzle.

ACROSS

1. Visceral muscle tissue
3. Adipose
8. Glands that release substances through ducts
9. Voluntary
10. Supporting cells of nervous system
11. Unusually thick scar
12. Cartilage cells

DOWN

2. Intracellular substance of a tissue
4. Carries nerve impulses away from the cell body
5. Many layers of epithelial cells
6. Most abundant tissue in body
7. Flat, scalelike epithelial cells

CHECK YOUR KNOWLEDGE

Labeling

Label the following images and identify the principal tissue type of each. Be as specific as possible. Consult your textbook if you need assistance.

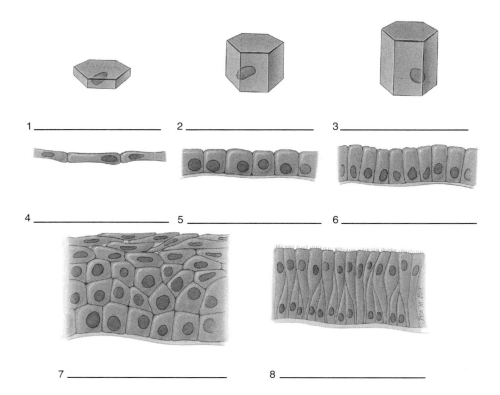

1 _____

2 _____

3 _____

4 _____

5 _____

6 _____

7 _____

8 _____

Multiple Choice

Circle the correct answer.

9. Which of the following is *not* an example of connective tissue?
   A. Striated
   B. Areolar
   C. Reticular
   D. Hematopoietic

10. Which of the following is the most abundant and widely distributed type of body tissue?
    A. Epithelial
    B. Connective
    C. Muscle
    D. Nerve

11. Simple, squamous epithelial tissue is made up of which of the following?
    A. A single layer of long, narrow cells
    B. Several layers of long, narrow cells
    C. A single layer of very thin and irregularly shaped cells
    D. Several layers of flat, scalelike cells

12. Which of the following groupings is correct when describing one of the muscle cell types?
    A. Visceral, striated, involuntary
    B. Skeletal, smooth, voluntary
    C. Cardiac, smooth, involuntary
    D. Skeletal, striated, voluntary

13. Which statement is *not* true regarding tissue repair?
    A. Skeletal muscle tissue rarely regenerates itself when injured.
    B. Tissues have varying capacity to repair themselves.
    C. Nerve tissue has limited capacity to regenerate.
    D. Neuroglia produce nerve growth factors that offer promise of treating brain damage.

Fill in the Blanks

14. _____ connective tissue is the "glue" that helps keep the organs of the body together.

15. Mucus-producing cells that appear in simple columnar epithelium are known as _____ cells.

16. The intracellular substance of a tissue is the _____.

17. The thick dark bands in cardiac muscle tissue are called _____ _____.

18. A _____ is an unusually thick scar that develops in the lower layer of skin.

19. The growth of new tissue after it has been damaged is accomplished by a process known as _____.

20. _____ _____ is a screening process used to match donors to recipients when performing organ transplants.

CHAPTER 5

Organ Systems of the Body

A smooth-running automobile is the result of many systems working together harmoniously. The engine, the fuel system, the exhaust system, the brake system, and the cooling system are but a few of the many complex structural units that the automobile as a whole relies on to keep it functioning smoothly. So it is with the human body. We, too, depend on the successful performance of many individual systems working together to create and maintain a healthy human being.

When you have completed your review of the 11 major organ systems and the organs that make up these systems, you will find your understanding of the performance of the body as a whole much more meaningful.

TOPICS FOR REVIEW

Before progressing to Chapter 6, you should have an understanding of the 11 major organ systems and be able to identify the organs that are included in each system. Your review should also include current approaches to organ replacement.

ORGAN SYSTEMS OF THE BODY

Match each term on the left with its corresponding term on the right.

Group A

_____ 1. Integumentary	A. Hair	
_____ 2. Skeletal	B. Spinal cord	
_____ 3. Muscular	C. Hormones	
_____ 4. Nervous	D. Tendons	
_____ 5. Endocrine	E. Ligaments	

Group B

_____ 6. Cardiovascular	A. Esophagus	
_____ 7. Lymphatic	B. Ureters	
_____ 8. Urinary	C. Larynx	
_____ 9. Digestive	D. Genitalia	
_____ 10. Respiratory	E. Spleen	
_____ 11. Reproductive	F. Capillaries	

Circle the word in each word group that does not belong.

12. Pharynx   Trachea   Mouth   Alveoli

13. Uterus   Rectum   Gonads   Prostate

14. Veins   Arteries   Heart   Pancreas

15. Pineal   Bladder   Ureters   Urethra

16. Tendon   Smooth   Joints   Voluntary

17. Pituitary   Brain   Spinal cord   Nerves

18. Cartilage   Joints   Ligaments   Tendons

19. Hormones   Pituitary   Pancreas   Appendix

20. Thymus   Nails   Hair   Oil glands

21. Esophagus   Pharynx   Mouth   Trachea

22. Thymus   Spleen   Tonsils   Liver

23. Fill in the missing areas.

SYSTEM	ORGANS	FUNCTIONS
1. Integumentary	Skin, nails, hair, sense receptors, sweat glands, oil glands	
2. Skeletal		Support, movement, storage of minerals, blood formation
3. Muscular	Muscles	
4.	Brain, spinal cord, nerves	Communication, integration, control, recognition of sensory stimuli
5. Endocrine		Secretion of hormones; communication, integration, control
6. Cardiovascular	Heart, blood vessels	
7. Lymphatic		Transportation, immune system
8.	Kidneys, ureters, bladder, urethra	Elimination of wastes, electrolyte balance, acid-base balance, water balance
9. Digestive		Digestion of food, absorption of nutrients
10.	Nose, pharynx, larynx, trachea, bronchi, lungs	Exchange of gases in the lungs
11. Reproductive		Survival of species; production of sex cells, fertilization, development, birth; nourishment of offspring; production of hormones

▶ *If you had difficulty with this section, review pages 89-100 and the chapter summary on pages 105-107.*

ORGAN REPLACEMENT AND TRANSPLANTATION

Fill in the blanks.

24. An organ not required for life to continue is a _____

   _____.

25. Many people suffering from deafness have had their hearing partially restored by "artificial ears" called

   _____   _____.

26. One of the earliest devices to augment vital functions was the "artificial kidney" or

   _____   _____.

27. Electromechanical devices that help keep blood pumping in patients suffering from end-stage heart

   disease are known as _____   _____   _____

   _____.

28. One approach that offers the hope of a permanent solution to loss of vital organ function is

   _____   _____.

29. After cancerous breasts are removed, "new" breasts can be formed from skin and muscle tissue using a

   method known as _____   _____   _____.

30. The advantage to using a patient's own tissues in organ replacement is that the possibility of

   _____ is reduced.

▶ *If you had difficulty with this section, review pages 100-105.*

UNSCRAMBLE THE WORDS

31. **RTAHE**

32. **IEPLNA**

33. **EENVR**

34. **SUHESOPGA**

Take the circled letters, unscramble
them, and fill in the statement.

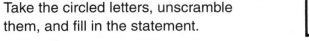

The more thoroughly you review this chapter, the less

35. [ ][ ][ ][ ][ ][ ][ ]   **you will be during your test.**

APPLYING WHAT YOU KNOW

36. Myrna is 15 years old and has not yet started menstruating. Her family physician decides to consult two other physicians, each of whom specializes in a different system. Specialists in the areas of

_____ and _____ were consulted.

37. Brian is admitted to the hospital with second- and third-degree burns over 50% of his body. He is placed in isolation. When Jenny visits him, she is required to wear a hospital gown and mask. Why is Brian placed in isolation? Why is Jenny required to wear special attire?

38. Sheila had a mastectomy to remove a cancerous lesion in her breast. Her body rejected the breast implant used to reconstruct her breast. Is there another breast reconstruction option that can be offered to Sheila? If so, explain this option.

39. Word Find

Find and circle the names of 11 organ systems. Words may be spelled top to bottom, bottom to top, right to left, left to right, or diagonally.

Circulatory
Digestive
Endocrine
Integumentary
Lymphatic
Muscular

Nervous
Reproductive
Respiratory
Skeletal
Urinary

```
Y R A T N E M U G E T N I R F
H N E R V O U S K I R J M G T
L Y M P H A T I C I S Y Y U I
B N X Y R O T A L U C R I C W
P E L R E O M J M S O M M P S
C C W M A N D L A T E L E K S
R R K E M L I U A A V V U K N
D K X P D J U R C J I R Q E M
C D B V C V I C C T T K W C X
X R Q Q D P H C S O I X P A Z
M F M U S Y D E V U D V Y K E
U E S E C Z G T Q D M N E K O
P Y R A N I R U C T C N E W H
N H T N D E P S I X A Q O I E
```

DID YOU KNOW?

- Muscles comprise 40% of your body weight. Your skeleton, however, only accounts for 18% of your body weight.
- The coccyx (tailbone) has no purpose today. Many scientists believe that it is what is left of the mammal tail that humans used to have in prehistoric years.

KNOW YOUR MEDICAL TERMS

True or False. Indicate in the blank space if the literal translation is true or false for the medical term.

_____ 40. adrenal gland   means   toward/kidney/acorn

_____ 41. digestive   means   stomach/pertaining

_____ 42. capillary   means   hair/relating to

_____ 43. feces   means   waste

_____ 44. hormone   means   excite

_____ 45. integument   means   on/center/result of action

_____ 46. kidney   means   womb

_____ 47. lymphatic   means   flesh/relating

_____ 48. organ   means   relating to system

_____ 49. stem cell   means   tree trunk/storeroom

_____ 50. radiography   means   frequency/drawing

 If you had difficulty with this section, review pages 90-92.

ORGAN SYSTEMS

Fill in the crossword puzzle.

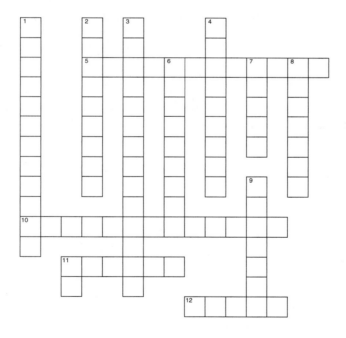

ACROSS
5. Specialized signal of nervous system (two words)
10. Skin
11. Testes and ovaries
12. Undigested residue of digestion

DOWN
1. Inflammation of the appendix
2. Vulva, penis, and scrotum
3. Heart and blood vessels
4. Subdivision of circulatory system
6. System of hormones
7. Waste product of kidneys
8. Agent that causes change in the activity of a structure
9. Chemical secretion of endocrine system
11. Gastrointestinal tract (abbreviation)

CHECK YOUR KNOWLEDGE

Multiple Choice

Circle the correct answer.

1. Which body system serves to clean the blood of waste products?
   A. Digestive
   B. Endocrine
   C. Cardiovascular
   D. Urinary

2. Ovaries and testes are considered components of which system?
   A. Reproductive system
   B. Endocrine system
   C. Both A and B
   D. None of the above

3. Which of the following organs is classified as an accessory organ of the digestive system?
   A. Mouth
   B. Esophagus
   C. Tongue
   D. Anal canal

4. Factors in the environment such as heat, light, pressure, and temperature that can be recognized by the nervous system are called:
   A. Effectors
   B. Stimuli
   C. Receptors
   D. Nerve impulses

5. Which body system stores the mineral calcium?
   A. Cardiovascular
   B. Digestive
   C. Lymphatic
   D. Skeletal

6. What is undigested material in the gastrointestinal tract called?
   A. Feces
   B. Urine
   C. Lymph
   D. Blood

7. Which body system produces heat and maintains body posture?
   A. Endocrine
   B. Muscular
   C. Cardiovascular
   D. Skeletal

8. Which of the following is *not* a function of the integumentary system?
   A. Integration
   B. Temperature regulation
   C. Ability to serve as a sense organ
   D. Protection

9. Which of the following is *not* a component of the digestive system?
   A. Spleen
   B. Liver
   C. Pancreas
   D. Gallbladder

10. When a group of tissues starts working together to perform a common function, what level of organization is achieved?
    A. Systemic
    B. Tissue
    C. Organ
    D. Cellular

Matching

Match each word in column A with the most appropriate corresponding word in column B. (There is only one correct answer for each.)

Column A

_____ 11. Sweat glands

_____ 12. Heart

_____ 13. Spleen

_____ 14. Vas deferens

_____ 15. Bladder

_____ 16. Gallbladder

_____ 17. Uterine tubes

_____ 18. Trachea

_____ 19. Spinal cord

_____ 20. Adrenals

Column B

A. Endocrine

B. Urinary

C. Integumentary

D. Cardiovascular

E. Respiratory

F. Digestive

G. Male reproductive

H. Lymphatic

I. Female reproductive

J. Nervous

CHAPTER 6

Mechanisms of Disease

One of our foremost concerns is health. We are fascinated and constantly confronted with information regarding what is necessary to be in good health, what is required for proper maintenance of the body, and what behaviors are responsible for disease.

Organisms play an important role in health. They are microscopic structures that are present everywhere. Many organisms are helpful and may be used for the preparation of foods, in industry and agriculture, to solve problems during the production of shelter and clothing, and in combating disease. However, many other organisms are responsible for producing disease. They attack and disturb the normal homeostasis of the body and adversely affect our health. Many varieties of organisms exist. They are often classified by shape, size, function, or staining properties. To prevent disease, we must prevent pathogenic or disease-producing organisms from entering the body. This is not an easy task because we are surrounded by pathogenic organisms. It is important that we understand the transmission and control of these organisms to fully comprehend the mechanisms of disease.

TOPICS FOR REVIEW

Before progressing to Chapter 7 you should familiarize yourself with disease terminology and patterns of disease. You should continue your review by studying pathophysiology and pathogenic organisms. Finally, an understanding of tumors, cancer, and inflammation is necessary to round out your knowledge of this chapter.

STUDYING DISEASE

Match each term on the left with its corresponding description on the right.

Group A

_____ 1. Pathology

_____ 2. Signs

_____ 3. Symptoms

_____ 4. Syndrome

_____ 5. Etiology

A. Subjective abnormalities

B. Study of disease

C. Collection of different signs and symptoms that present a clear picture of a pathological condition

D. Study of factors involved in causing a disease

E. Objective abnormalities

Group B

_____ 6. Latent   A. Recovery
_____ 7. Convalescence   B. Disease native to a local region
_____ 8. Pandemics   C. "Hidden" stage
_____ 9. Endemic   D. Epidemics that spread throughout the world
_____ 10. Pathogenesis   E. Actual pattern of a disease's development

▶ *If you had difficulty with this section, review pages 110-116.*

PATHOPHYSIOLOGY

Fill in the blanks.

11. _____ is the organized study of the underlying physiological processes associated with disease.

12. Many diseases are best understood as disturbances of _____.

13. Altered or _____ genes can cause abnormal proteins to be made.

14. An organism that lives in or on another organism to obtain its nutrients is called a

_____.

15. Abnormal tissue growths may also be referred to as _____.

16. *Autoimmunity* literally means _____.

17. Genetic factors, age, lifestyle, stress, environmental factors, and preexisting conditions are

_____ _____ that may be responsible for predisposing a person to disease.

18. Scientists at the _____ _____

_____ _____ continuously track the incidence and spread of disease in this country and worldwide.

19. Conditions caused by psychological factors are sometimes called _____ disorders.

20. A primary condition can put a person at risk for developing a _____ condition.

▶ *If you had difficulty with this section, review pages 116-117.*

PATHOGENIC ORGANISMS

Circle the correct answer.

21. The smallest of all pathogens—microscopic nonliving particles—are called:
    A. Bacteria
    B. Fungi
    C. Viruses
    D. Protozoa

22. A tiny, primitive cell without a nucleus is called a:
    A. Bacterium
    B. Fungus
    C. Virus
    D. Protozoa

23. An example of a viral disease is:
    A. Diarrhea
    B. Mononucleosis
    C. Syphilis
    D. Toxic shock syndrome

24. Bacteria that require oxygen for metabolism are classified as:
    A. Gram positive
    B. Gram negative
    C. Aerobic
    D. Anaerobic

25. Bacilli are shaped like:
    A. Spheres
    B. Curves
    C. Squares
    D. Rods

26. Without chlorophyll, _____ cannot produce their own food, so they must consume or parasitize other organisms.
    A. Bacteria
    B. Fungi
    C. Viruses
    D. Protozoa

27. Protozoa include:
    A. Amoebas
    B. Flagellates
    C. Ciliates
    D. All of the above

28. Pathogenic animals include which of the following?
    A. Nematodes
    B. Platyhelminths
    C. Arthropods
    D. All of the above

29. The key to preventing diseases caused by pathogenic organisms is to:
    A. Have an annual physical
    B. Stop them from entering the body
    C. Isolate yourself from all disease-carrying individuals
    D. None of the above

30. The destruction of all living organisms is known as:
    A. Disinfection
    B. Antisepsis
    C. Sterilization
    D. Isolation

31. Ways in which pathogens can spread include:
    A. Person-to-person contact
    B. Environmental contact
    C. Opportunistic invasion
    D. Transmission by vector
    E. All of the above

32. Compounds produced by certain living organisms that kill or inhibit pathogens are:
    A. Antiseptics
    B. Antibiotics
    C. Disinfectants
    D. Sterilizers

 If you had difficulty with this section, review pages 117-128.

TUMORS AND CANCER

Circle the correct answer.

33. Benign tumors usually grow (*slowly* or *quickly*).

34. Malignant tumors (*are* or *are not*) encapsulated.

35. An example of a benign tumor that arises from epithelial tissue is a (*papilloma* or *lipoma*).

36. A general term for malignant tumors that arise from connective tissues is (*melanoma* or *sarcoma*).

37. Abnormal, undifferentiated tumor cells are often produced by a process called (*hyperplasia* or *anaplasia*).

38. A cancer specialist is an (*osteologist* or *oncologist*).

39. The Papanicolaou test is a (*biopsy* or *MRI*).

40. (*Staging* or *Grading*) involves classifying a tumor based on its size and the extent of its spread.

41. Cachexia involves a loss of (*appetite* or *hair*).

▷ *If you had difficulty with this section, review pages 128-133.*

WARNING SIGNS OF CANCER

List the eight warning signs of cancer.

42. _____

43. _____

44. _____

45. _____

46. _____

47. _____

48. _____

49. _____

▷ *If you had difficulty with this section, review page 131.*

INFLAMMATION

If the statement is true, write "T" in the answer blank. If the statement is false, correct the statement by circling the incorrect term and writing the correct term in the answer blank.

_____ 50. As tissue cells are damaged, they release inflammation mediators such as histamines, prostaglandins, and kinins.

_____ 51. Inflammatory exudate is quickly removed by lymphatic vessels and carried to lymph nodes, which act as filters.

_____ 52. Inflammation mediators can also act as signals that attract red blood cells to the injury site.

_____ 53. The movement of white blood cells in response to chemical attractants is called *chemotaxis*.

_____ 54. Inflammation can be local or systemic.

_____ 55. Fevers usually subside after the irritant has been eliminated.

_____ 56. The fever response in children and in older adults often differs from that in the normal adult.

▷ *If you had difficulty with this section, review pages 133-135.*

UNSCRAMBLE THE WORDS

57. **N G F U I**

[ ][ ][ ][○][○]

58. **C E O N O G N E**

[ ][○][ ][○][ ][ ][ ]

59. **A D E E M**

[ ][○][ ][○]

60. **R S P O E**

[ ][ ][ ][○]

Take the circled letters, unscramble
them, and fill in the solution.

What Mr. Lynch found to be most difficult as a teacher.

61. [ ][ ][ ][ ][ ][ ][ ][ ]

APPLYING WHAT YOU KNOW

62. Trent was examined by his doctor and was diagnosed as having a rhinovirus. Does he have need for concern? Why or why not?

63. Julius, a 2-year-old child, was experiencing rectal itching and insomnia. The pediatrician told Julius' mother that he suspected a nematode. What is the common term for the specific nematode that might cause these symptoms?

64. Shirley was cleaning her house and wanted to use the most appropriate and effective aseptic method to prevent the spread of germs. What would you suggest?

65. Mr. and Mrs. Gibbs adopted a child of Chinese descent. Mrs. Gibbs researched the "gene pool" of the child to alert her to any special concerns. What is a "gene pool" and how will this information assist Mr. and Mrs. Gibbs in the rearing of their child?

66. Bill has decided to become a paramedic. When he applied for school, it was suggested that he receive the series of vaccinations for hepatitis B. Why?

67. Word Find

Find and circle 18 terms presented in this chapter. Words may be spelled top to bottom, bottom to top, right to left, left to right, or diagonally.

```
N  P  E  S  D  B  S  L  A  A  C  E  R
W  O  L  S  I  C  I  M  E  D  I  P  E
X  V  I  O  F  S  X  V  R  E  N  A  T
O  D  P  T  U  E  A  D  O  N  C  R  U
H  S  O  V  A  S  T  T  P  O  U  A  C
Y  S  M  P  U  M  O  A  S  M  B  S  A
Y  P  A  R  O  I  M  B  I  A  A  I  I
N  L  I  O  S  R  E  A  F  L  T  T  D
W  V  J  T  C  Z  H  C  L  L  I  E  Y
W  Q  K  O  W  G  C  T  Q  F  O  C  M
V  Q  F  Z  I  F  G  E  R  P  N  F  A
K  E  N  O  Q  E  J  R  B  A  F  I  L
B  B  J  A  F  E  N  I  C  C  A  V  H
W  Z  F  H  R  B  S  U  D  M  Q  D  C
M  X  E  C  K  M  B  M  K  U  O  Z  P
```

Acute	Chlamydia	Metastasis
Adenoma	Ciliate	Parasite
Arthropod	Epidemic	Protozoa
Bacterium	Incubation	Spore
Biopsy	Inflammation	Vaccine
Chemotaxis	Lipoma	Virus

DID YOU KNOW?

- As many as 500,000 Americans die from cancer each year, making it the second-leading cause of death after cardiovascular disease. Half of all cancers are diagnosed in people under the age of 67.

- Scientists have proved that stress can change the bacteria levels in the gut which can have significant impact on our immunity.

- Israeli scientists have discovered that bacteria can communicate with each other through nanotubes.

KNOW YOUR MEDICAL TERMS

Circle the correct answer.

68. patho   means   (*health* or *disease*)

69. edema   means   (*swelling* or *broad*)

70. amoeba   means   (*change* or *small*)

71. fungus   means   (*mold* or *mushroom*)

72. pus   means   (*rotten* or *stringy*)

73. anthrax   means   (*boil* or *cow*)

74. acute   means   (*quick* or *sharp*)

▶ *If you had difficulty with this section, review pages 112-115.*

MECHANISMS OF DISEASE

Fill in the crossword puzzle.

ACROSS

4. Roundworm
7. Microscopic organism
8. Round cells
10. Possess pseudopodia
11. Rod-shaped cells

DOWN

1. Tissue swelling
2. Lack chlorophyll
3. Glandular cancer
5. "Cancer gene"
6. Spreads disease to other organisms
9. Thick inflammatory exudate

CHECK YOUR KNOWLEDGE

Multiple Choice

Circle the correct answer.

1. Diseases with undetermined causes are:
   A. Asymptomatic
   B. Idiopathic
   C. Psychogenic
   D. Predisposing

2. The study of the occurrence, distribution, and transmission of diseases is:
   A. Entomology
   B. Pathology
   C. Oncology
   D. Epidemiology

3. Streptomycin is an example of a/an:
   A. Antibiotic
   B. Vaccine
   C. Pathogenic organism
   D. All of the above

4. Reversal of a chronic condition is called:
   A. Inflammatory response
   B. Predisposing condition
   C. Hemostasis
   D. Remission

5. If antibodies are found in an immunological test, it is assumed that:
   A. The patient has been exposed to a pathogen
   B. The infection is gone
   C. A and B
   D. None of the above

6. An epidemiologist:
   A. Studies the transmission of disease
   B. Monitors infection control programs
   C. Tracks the spread of disease
   D. All of the above

7. Study of the underlying physiological processes associated with disease leads to:
   A. Strategies of prevention
   B. Strategies of treatment
   C. A and B
   D. None of the above

8. Severe loss of appetite, weight loss, and general weakness in a cancer patient describe:
   A. Secondary infection
   B. Cachexia
   C. Inflammatory response
   D. Chemotaxis

9. Intracellular parasites that are not technically living organisms are characteristics of:
   A. Bacteria
   B. Fungi
   C. Amoebas
   D. Viruses

10. Examples of protozoa include all of the following *except*:
    A. Bacilli
    B. Flagellates
    C. Sporozoa
    D. Amoebas

Matching

Match each term in column A with the most appropriate definition or description in column B. (Only one answer is correct for each.)

Column A

_____ 11. Syndrome

_____ 12. Metastasis

_____ 13. Anaerobic

_____ 14. Protozoa

_____ 15. Pathogenesis

_____ 16. Fever

_____ 17. Metazoa

_____ 18. Pathology

_____ 19. Neoplasm

_____ 20. Arthropods

Column B

A. Study of disease

B. Require absence of oxygen

C. Collection of signs and symptoms

D. Spread of cancer cells

E. Multicellular organisms that parasitize humans

F. Abnormal cell growth

G. Pattern of disease development

H. Mites

I. Inflammatory response

J. One-celled organisms that parasitize cells

MAJOR GROUPS OF PATHOGENIC BACTERIA

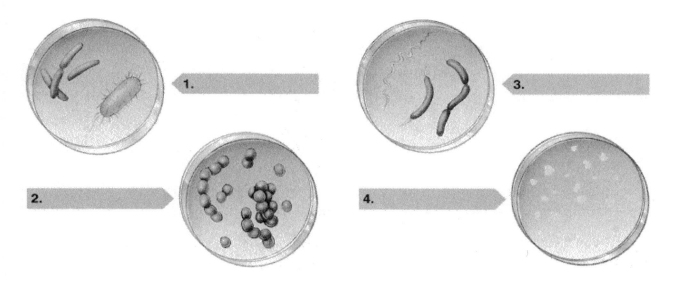

MAJOR GROUPS OF PATHOGENIC PROTOZOA

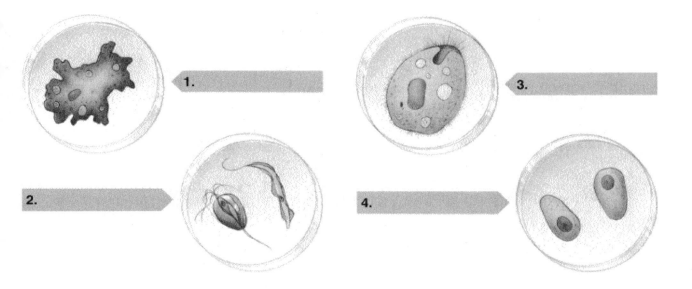

EXAMPLES OF PATHOGENIC ANIMALS

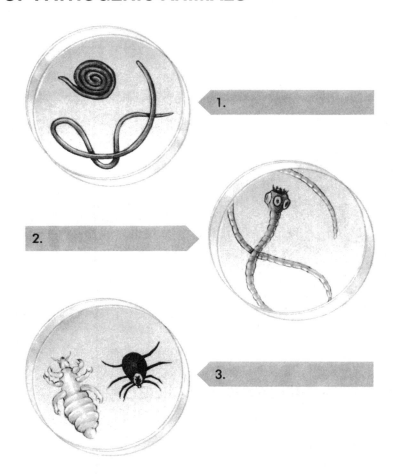

1.

2.

3.

MAJOR GROUPS OF PATHOGENIC FUNGI

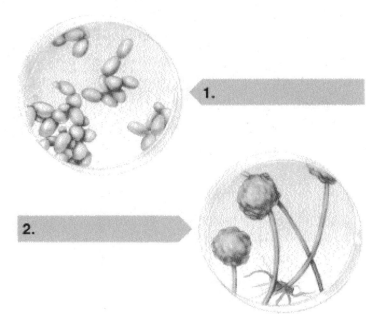

1.

2.

62. Word Find

Find and circle 15 terms presented in this chapter. Words may be spelled top to bottom, bottom to top, right to left, left to right, or diagonally.

Apocrine
Blister
Cuticle
Dehydration
Depilatories
Epidermis
Follicle
Lanugo

Lunula
Melanocyte
Mucus
Peritoneum
Pleurisy
Serous
Sudoriferous

```
S U D O R I F E R O U S V K R
E J U Q U E S T E C N O H Y U
I S J L M E L A N O C Y T E H
R I M U E N O T I R E P H S B
O M K N V A S T R L A N U G O
T R G U F G A U C E G O V W D
A E A L P R D I O N T F D R N
L D V A D M L C P D H S L Z F
I I N Y N L R L A M E N I R E
P P H Q O N E U X R R F E L G
E E Z F J U M Y O U U O C C B
D Z P E R J Y U V F C I I E O
G J S I W J S K C D T N O Z C
C O S M Z M F I B U G U X O J
X Y P M E I W E C V S U G B I
```

KNOW YOUR MEDICAL TERMS

Match the correct term with the literal translation below.

a. arrector
b. kera
c. append
d. lanugo
e. papilla

f. integ
g. bursa
h. sclero
i. alb
j. dermis

k. sudo
l. melan
m. stratum

63. _____ raiser

64. _____ down

65. _____ purse

66. _____ hang upon

67. _____ skin

68. _____ nipple

69. _____ layer

70. _____ sweat

71. _____ on/cover

72. _____ white

73. _____ hard

74. _____ horn

75. _____ black

▶ *If you had difficulty with this section, review pages 142-144.*

DID YOU KNOW?

- Because the dead cells of the epidermis are constantly being worn and washed away, we get a new outer skin layer every 27 days.
- A large amount of the dust in your home is actually dead skin.
- Humans shed about 600,000 particles of skin every hour or about 1.5 pounds a year. By age 70, an average person will have lost 105 pounds of skin!

SKIN/BODY MEMBRANES

Fill in the crossword puzzle.

ACROSS

1. Inflammation of the serous membrane that lines the chest and covers the lungs
4. Cutaneous
9. Membrane that lines joint spaces
10. "Goose pimples" (two words)
11. Cushionlike sacs found between moving body parts
12. Deeper of the two primary skin layers

DOWN

1. Forms the lining of serous body cavities
2. Oil gland
3. Bluish-gray color of skin due to decreased oxygen
5. Tough waterproof substance that protects body from excess fluid loss
6. Sweat gland
7. Brown pigment
8. Covers the surface of organs found in serous body cavities

CHECK YOUR KNOWLEDGE

Multiple Choice

Circle the correct answer.

1. What type of serous membrane that covers organs is found in all body cavities?
   A. Visceral
   B. Pleural
   C. Parietal
   D. Synovial

2. Which of the following statements about synovial membranes is true?
   A. They are classified as epithelial.
   B. They line joints.
   C. They contain a parietal layer.
   D. All of the above are true.

LONGITUDINAL SECTION OF THE SKIN

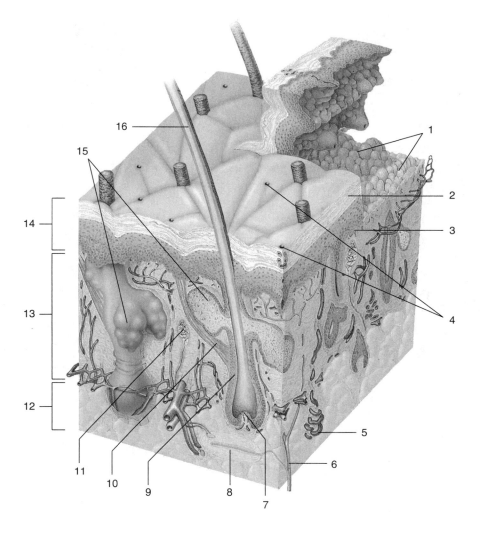

1. _____

2. _____

3. _____

4. _____

5. _____

6. _____

7. _____

8. _____

9. _____

10. _____

11. _____

12. _____

13. _____

14. _____

15. _____

16. _____

"RULE OF NINES" FOR ESTIMATING SKIN SURFACE BURNED

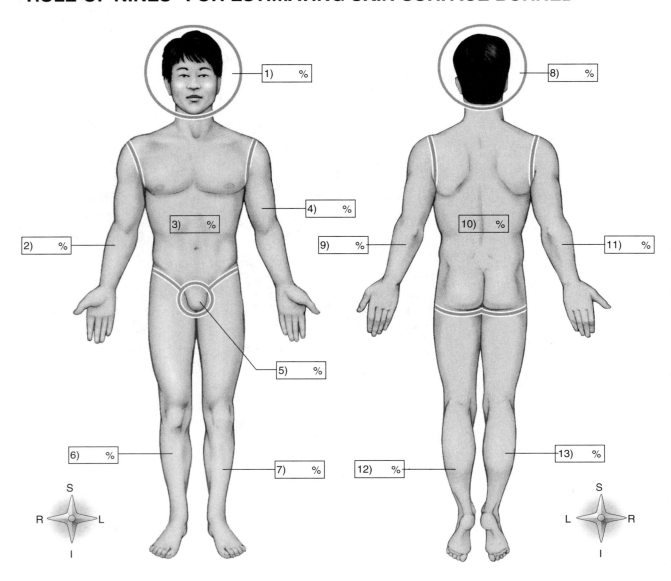

Circle the word in each word group that does not belong.

50. Cervical	Thoracic	Coxal	Coccyx
51. Pelvic girdle	Ankle	Wrist	Axial
52. Frontal	Occipital	Maxilla	Sphenoid
53. Scapula	Pectoral girdle	Ribs	Clavicle
54. Malleus	Vomer	Incus	Stapes
55. Ulna	Ilium	Ischium	Pubis
56. Carpal	Phalanges	Metacarpal	Ethmoid
57. Ethmoid	Parietal	Occipital	Nasal
58. Anvil	Atlas	Axis	Cervical

 If you had difficulty with this section, review pages 177-190.

DIFFERENCES BETWEEN A MAN'S AND A WOMAN'S SKELETON

Identify each skeletal structure as being typically male or female.

A.   Male   B.   Female

_____ 59. Funnel-shaped pelvis

_____ 60. Broader-shaped pelvis

_____ 61. Wider pubic angle

_____ 62. Larger coxal bones

_____ 63. Wider pelvic inlet

 If you had difficulty with this section, review page 190.

BONE MARKINGS

From the choices given, match each bone with its identification marking. Answer choices may be used more than once.

A. Mastoid
B. Pterygoid process
C. Foramen magnum
D. Sella turcica
E. Mental foramen
F. Conchae
G. Xiphoid process

H. Glenoid cavity
I. Olecranon process
J. Ischium
K. Acetabulum
L. Symphysis pubis
M. Ilium
N. Greater trochanter

O. Medial malleolus
P. Calcaneus
Q. Acromion process
R. Frontal sinuses
S. Condyloid process
T. Tibial tuberosity

_____ 64. Occipital

_____ 65. Sternum

_____ 66. Coxal

_____ 67. Femur

_____ 68. Ulna

_____ 69. Temporal

_____ 70. Tarsals

_____ 71. Sphenoid

_____ 72. Ethmoid

_____ 73. Scapula

_____ 74. Tibia

_____ 75. Frontal

_____ 76. Mandible

 If you had difficulty with this section, review pages 179-189.

JOINTS (ARTICULATIONS)

Circle the correct answer.

77. Freely movable joints are (*amphiarthroses* or *diarthroses*).

78. The sutures in the skull are (*synarthrotic* or *amphiarthrotic*) joints.

79. All (*diarthrotic* or *amphiarthrotic*) joints have a joint capsule, a joint cavity, and a layer of cartilage over the ends of the two joining bones.

80. (*Ligaments* or *Tendons*) grow out of periosteum and attach two bones together.

81. The (*articular cartilage* or *epiphyseal cartilage*) absorbs jolts.

82. Gliding joints are the (*least movable* or *most movable*) of the diarthrotic joints.

83. The knee is the (*largest* or *smallest*) joint.

84. Hinge joints allow motion in (*2* or *4*) directions.

85. The saddle joint at the base of each of our thumbs allows for greater (*strength* or *mobility*).

86. When you rotate your head, you are using a (*gliding* or *pivot*) joint.

▶ *If you had difficulty with this section, review pages 191-194.*

SKELETAL DISORDERS

Fill in the blanks.

87. _____ is an imaging technique that allows a physician to examine the internal structure of a joint without the use of extensive surgery.

88. One of the most common skeletal tumors and one of the most rapidly fatal is

_____.

89. _____ is the name of a common disorder in which bones lose minerals and become less dense.

90. A metabolic disorder involving mineral loss in bones due to a lack of vitamin D is

_____.

91. A metabolic disorder that is often asymptomatic and affects older adults is

_____ _____.

92. The general name for bacterial infections of bone and marrow tissue is

_____.

93. Closed fractures, also known as _____

_____, do not pierce the skin.

94. _____ _____ are breaks that produce many fragments.

95. The most common noninflammatory joint disease is _____ or

_____ _____

_____.

96. Three major types of arthritis are _____,

_____, and _____.

97. One form of infectious arthritis, _____

_____, was identified in 1975 in Connecticut and has since spread
across the continent.

▷ *If you had difficulty with this section, review pages 194-202.*

UNSCRAMBLE THE BONES

98. **E T V E R R B A E**

99. **B P S U I**

100. **S C A L U P A**

101. **I M D B A L N E**

102. **A P N H G A E L S**

Take the circled letters, unscramble
them, and fill in the solution.

What the fat lady wore to the ball.

103.

APPLYING WHAT YOU KNOW

104. Mrs. Perine had advanced cancer of the bone. As the disease progressed, Mrs. Perine required several
blood transfusions throughout the time she was receiving therapy. She asked the doctor one day to
explain the necessity for the transfusions. What explanation might the doctor give to Mrs. Perine?

105. Dr. Kennedy, an orthopedic surgeon, called the admissions office of the hospital and advised that he would be admitting a patient in the next hour with an epiphyseal fracture. Without any other information, the patient is assigned to the pediatric ward. What prompted this assignment?

106. Mrs. Van Skiver, age 75, noticed when she went in for her physical examination that she was a half inch shorter than she was on her last visit. Dr. Veazey suggested she begin a regimen of dietary supplements of calcium, vitamin D, and a prescription for sex hormone therapy. What bone disease did Dr. Veazey suspect?

107. Mr. Ferber was moving and experienced severe sharp pain in his lower back while lifting some boxes. The pain was not relieved by traditional home remedies or pain medication. He finally sought the advice of a physician after being unable to relieve the pain for 48 hours. What might be a possible diagnosis?

108. Word Find

Find and circle 13 terms presented in this chapter. Words may be spelled top to bottom, bottom to top, right to left, left to right, or diagonally.

Amphiarthroses	Lacunae
Articulation	Osteoblasts
Axial	Osteoclasts
Canaliculi	Periosteum
Compact	Sinus
Fontanels	Trabeculae
Hematopoiesis	

```
S A N A R T I C U L A T I O N
I O M P L T C A P M O C E S C
M H E P T T A M A S A I A T P
O E L F H T A E P N I F L E T
S M L A S I E I A O O P U O S
S A M O I L A L O N I E C B T
E T S U N X I R T R A T E L S
S O B T E C A A T N A E B A A
R P I E U T N E U H O O A S L
S O T L C E S C T A R S R T C
U I I R L O A O O A O T S O
N E T S H L T A I R I I S A E
I S T H E U O A M R C X S E T
S I S T A I E T C R E S I A S
L S C A S H S T O I O P T S O
```

DID YOU KNOW?

- The bones of the hands and feet make up more than half of the total 206 bones of the body.
- You are taller in the morning. Throughout the day the cartilage between your bones is compressed, making you about 1 cm shorter by the end of the day.
- The bones of the middle ear are mature at birth.

POSTERIOR VIEW OF SKELETON

1. _____

2. _____

3. _____

4. _____

5. _____

6. _____

7. _____

8. _____

9. _____

10. _____

11. _____

12. _____

13. _____

14. _____

15. _____

16. _____

17. _____

18. _____

19. _____

20. _____

21. _____

22. _____

23. _____

24. _____

25. _____

26. _____

27. _____

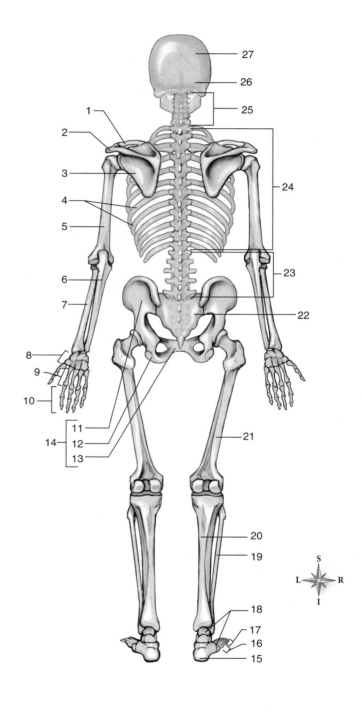

SKULL VIEWED FROM THE RIGHT SIDE

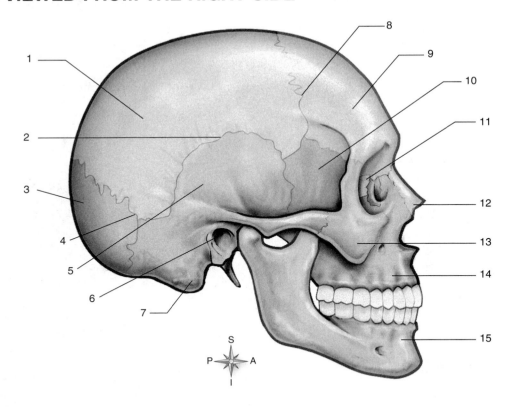

1. _____

2. _____

3. _____

4. _____

5. _____

6. _____

7. _____

8. _____

9. _____

10. _____

11. _____

12. _____

13. _____

14. _____

15. _____

SKULL VIEWED FROM THE FRONT

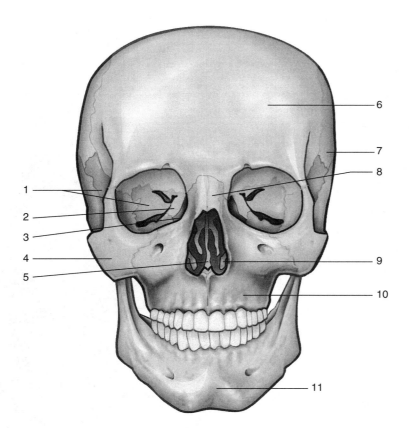

1. _____   7. _____

2. _____   8. _____

3. _____   9. _____

4. _____   10. _____

5. _____   11. _____

6. _____

STRUCTURE OF A DIARTHROTIC JOINT

1. _____

2. _____

3. _____

4. _____

5. _____

6. _____

7. _____

8. _____

9. _____

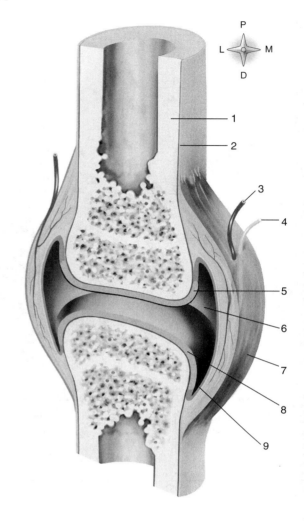

FUNCTIONS OF SKELETAL MUSCLE

Fill in the blanks.

21. Muscles move bones by _____ on them.

22. As a rule, only the _____ bone moves.

23. The _____ bone moves toward the
_____ bone.

24. Of all the muscles contracting simultaneously, the one mainly responsible for producing a
particular movement is called the _____
_____ for that movement.

25. As prime movers contract, other muscles called _____ relax.

26. The biceps brachii is the prime mover during flexing, and the brachialis is its helper or
_____ muscle.

27. We are able to maintain our body position because of a specialized type of skeletal muscle contraction
called _____ _____.

28. _____ _____ maintains body
posture by counteracting the pull of gravity.

29. A decrease in temperature, a condition known as _____, will
drastically affect cellular activity and normal body function.

30. Energy required to produce a muscle contraction is obtained from
_____.

▶ *If you had difficulty with this section, review pages 215-217.*

FATIGUE
ROLE OF OTHER BODY SYSTEMS
MOTOR UNIT
MUSCLE STIMULUS

If the statement is true, write "T" in the answer blank. If the statement is false, correct the statement by circling the incorrect term and writing the correct term in the answer blank.

_____ 31. The point of contact between the nerve ending and the muscle fiber is called
a *motor neuron.*

_____ 32. A motor neuron together with the cells it innervates is called a *motor unit.*

_____ 33. If muscle cells are stimulated repeatedly without adequate periods of rest,
the strength of the muscle contraction will decrease, resulting in fatigue.

_____ 34. The depletion of oxygen in muscle cells during vigorous and prolonged
exercise is known as *fatigue.*

_____ 35. An adequate stimulus will contract a muscle cell completely because of the "must" theory.

_____ 36. When oxygen supplies run low, muscle cells produce ATP and other waste products during contraction.

_____ 37. In a laboratory setting, a single muscle fiber can be isolated and subjected to stimuli of varying intensities so that it can be studied.

_____ 38. The minimal level of stimulation required to cause a fiber to contract is called the _threshold stimulus_.

_____ 39. Smooth muscles bring about movements by pulling on bones across movable joints.

_____ 40. A nervous system disorder that shuts off impulses to certain skeletal muscles may result in paralysis.

TYPES OF SKELETAL MUSCLE CONTRACTION

Circle the correct answer.

41. When a muscle contracts and no movement results, the contraction is:
    A. Isometric
    B. Isotonic
    C. Twitch
    D. Tetanic

42. Walking is an example of which type of contraction?
    A. Isometric
    B. Isotonic
    C. Twitch
    D. Tetanic

43. Pushing against a wall is an example of which type of contraction?
    A. Isotonic
    B. Isometric
    C. Twitch
    D. Tetanic

44. Endurance training is also known as:
    A. Isometrics
    B. Hypertrophy
    C. Aerobic training
    D. Strength training

45. Benefits of regular exercise include all of the following _except_:
    A. Improved lung functioning
    B. More efficient heart
    C. Less fatigue
    D. Atrophy

46. Twitch contractions easily can be seen:
    A. In isolated muscles prepared for research
    B. In a great deal of normal muscle activity
    C. During resting periods
    D. None of the above

47. Individual contractions "melt" together to produce a sustained contraction or:
    A. Twitch
    B. Tetanus
    C. Isotonic response
    D. Isometric response

48. In most cases, isotonic contraction of muscle produces movement at a/an:
    A. Insertion
    B. Beginning
    C. Joint
    D. Bursa

49. Prolonged inactivity causes muscles to shrink in mass, a condition called:
    A. Hypertrophy
    B. Disuse atrophy
    C. Paralysis
    D. Muscle fatigue

50. Muscle hypertrophy can be best enhanced by a program of:
    A. Isotonic exercise
    B. Better posture
    C. High-protein diet
    D. Strength training

▶ _If you had difficulty with this section, review pages 217-223._

78.   Word Find

Find and circle 25 muscle terms. Words may be spelled top to bottom, bottom to top, right to left, left to right, or diagonally.

```
G A S T R O C N E M I U S D U
M S G I O N O I S N E T X E U
U R N N T O M S R B S F D T T
S U I S C I B O N T P N E A R
C B R E U X V T O O E C L I A
L Q T R D E C O D A C M T R P
E T S T B L M N N V I E O T E
X F M I A F Y I E Y B N I S Z
S I A O V I E C T L S S D I I
S Y H N S S R O T A T O R G U
U A M G A R H P A I D J N R S
E H A T R O P H Y L N J T E B
L N O H T D E U G I T A F N T
O R I G I N O S N V S B Z Y L
S B V T O J C T R I C E P S S
```

Abductor	Flexion	Soleus
Atrophy	Gastrocnemius	Striated
Biceps	Hamstrings	Synergist
Bursa	Insertion	Tendon
Deltoid	Isometric	Tenosynovitis
Diaphragm	Isotonic	Trapezius
Dorsiflexion	Muscle	Triceps
Extension	Origin	
Fatigue	Rotator	

KNOW YOUR MEDICAL TERMS

Fill in the blanks.

79. mus _____   cle _____

80. myo _____   fila _____   ment _____

81. gastro _____   cnemius _____

82. pector _____   alis _____   major _____

83. posture _____

84. rigor _____   mortis _____

85. syn _____   erg _____   ist _____

▶ *If you had difficulty with this section, review pages 210 and 211.*

DID YOU KNOW?

- If all of your muscles pulled in one direction, you would have the power to move 25 tons.
- When you take a step, you are using up to 200 muscles. Walking uses a great deal of muscle power and is good exercise.
- Compared to its size, the tongue is the strongest muscle in your body.

THE MUSCULAR SYSTEM

Fill in the crossword puzzle.

ACROSS

2. Shaking your head "no"
6. Muscle shrinkage
7. Toward the body's midline
9. Produces movement opposite to prime movers
12. Movement that makes joint angles larger
13. Small fluid-filled sac between tendons and bones

DOWN

1. Increase in size
3. Away from the body's midline
4. Turning your palm from an anterior to posterior position
5. Attachment to the more movable bone
7. Protein which composes myofilaments
8. Attachment to the more stationary bone
10. Assists prime movers with movement
11. Anchors muscles to bones

MUSCLES—ANTERIOR VIEW

1. _____

2. _____

3. _____

4. _____

5. _____

6. _____

7. _____

8. _____

9. _____

10. _____

11. _____

12. _____

13. _____

14. _____

15. _____

16. _____

17. _____

18. _____

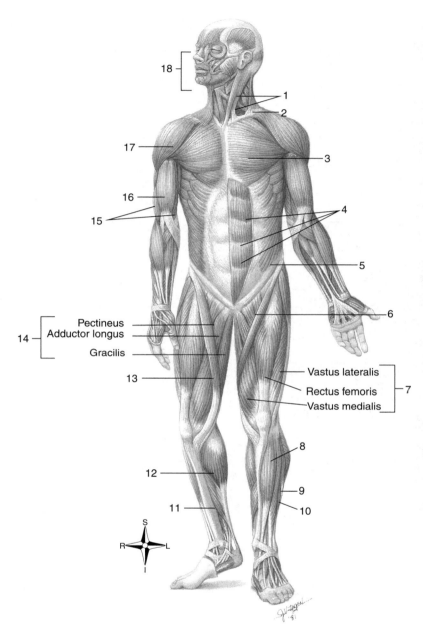

18

1

2

17

16

15

4

5

6

Pectineus
Adductor longus
14
Gracilis

13

Vastus lateralis
Rectus femoris   7
Vastus medialis

8

9

12

10

11

S
R — L
I

3

MUSCLES—POSTERIOR VIEW

1. _____

2. _____

3. _____

4. _____

5. _____

6. _____

7. _____

8. _____

9. _____

10. _____

11. _____

12. _____

13. _____

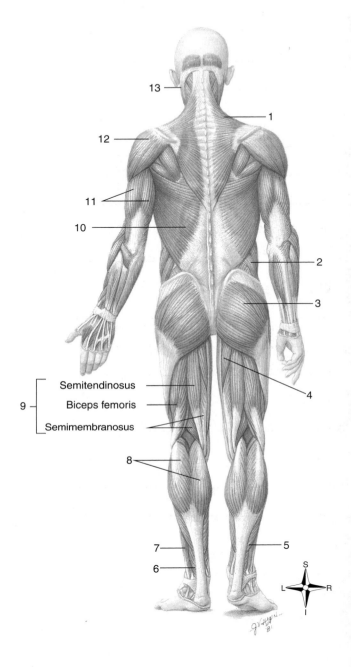

9 ⎡ Semitendinosus
  ⎢ Biceps femoris
  ⎣ Semimembranosus

CRANIAL NERVES

SPINAL NERVES

Match each of the numbered words with cranial or spinal nerves as appropriate and write the corresponding letter in the answer blank.

A. Cranial nerves   B. Spinal nerves

_____ 79. 12 pairs

_____ 80. Dermatome

_____ 81. Vagus

_____ 82. Shingles

_____ 83. 31 pairs

_____ 84. Optic

_____ 85. C1

_____ 86. Plexus

▷ *If you had difficulty with this section, review pages 263-268.*

AUTONOMIC NERVOUS SYSTEM

Match each term on the left with the appropriate description on the right.

_____ 87. Autonomic nervous system

_____ 88. Autonomic neurons

_____ 89. Preganglionic neurons

_____ 90. Visceral effectors

_____ 91. Sympathetic nervous system

_____ 92. Somatic nervous system

A. Divisions of ANS

B. Tissues to which autonomic neurons conduct impulses

C. Voluntary actions

D. Regulates body's involuntary functions

E. Motor neurons that make up the ANS

F. Conduct impulses between the spinal cord and a ganglion

SYMPATHETIC NERVOUS SYSTEM

PARASYMPATHETIC NERVOUS SYSTEM

Circle the correct answer.

93. Dendrites and cell bodies of sympathetic preganglionic neurons are located in the:
    A. Brainstem and sacral portion of the spinal cord
    B. Sympathetic ganglia
    C. Gray matter of the thoracic and upper lumbar segments of the spinal cord
    D. Ganglia close to effectors

94. Which of the following is *not* correct?
    A. Sympathetic preganglionic neurons have their cell bodies located in the lateral gray column of certain parts of the spinal cord.
    B. Sympathetic preganglionic axons pass along the dorsal root of certain spinal nerves.
    C. There are synapses within sympathetic ganglia.
    D. Sympathetic responses are usually widespread, involving many organs.

95. Another name for the parasympathetic nervous system is:
    A. Thoracolumbar
    B. Craniosacral
    C. Visceral
    D. ANS
    E. Cholinergic

96. Which statement is *not* correct?
    A. Sympathetic postganglionic neurons have their dendrites and cell bodies in sympathetic ganglia or collateral ganglia.
    B. Sympathetic ganglia are located in front of and at each side of the spinal column.
    C. Separate autonomic nerves distribute many sympathetic postganglionic axons to various internal organs.
    D. Very few sympathetic preganglionic axons synapse with postganglionic neurons.

97. Sympathetic stimulation usually results in a/an:
    A. Response by numerous organs
    B. Response by only one organ
    C. Increase in peristalsis
    D. Constriction of pupils

98. Parasympathetic stimulation frequently results in a/an:
    A. Response by only one organ
    B. Response by numerous organs
    C. Fight-or-flight syndrome
    D. Increase in heartbeat

Match each numbered description to its related nervous control system and write the corresponding letter in the answer blank.

A. Sympathetic control   B. Parasympathetic control

_____ 99. Constricts pupils

_____ 100. "Goose pimples"

_____ 101. Increases sweat secretion

_____ 102. Increases secretion of digestive juices

_____ 103. Constricts blood vessels

_____ 104. Slows heartbeat

_____ 105. Relaxes bladder

_____ 106. Increases epinephrine secretion

_____ 107. Increases peristalsis

_____ 108. Stimulates lens for near vision

▷ *If you had difficulty with this section, review pages 268-271.*

AUTONOMIC NEUROTRANSMITTERS

AUTONOMIC NERVOUS SYSTEM AS A WHOLE

Fill in the blanks.

109. Sympathetic preganglionic axons release the neurotransmitter _____.

110. Axons that release norepinephrine are classified as _____

_____.

111. Axons that release acetylcholine are classified as _____

_____.

112. The function of the autonomic nervous system is to regulate the body's involuntary functions in ways that maintain or restore _____.

113. Your _____ _____ is determined by the combined forces of the sympathetic and parasympathetic nervous systems.

114. According to some physiologists, meditation leads to _____ sympathetic activity and changes opposite to those of the fight-or-flight response.

115. _____ is a malignant tumor of the sympathetic nervous system.

▷ *If you had difficulty with this section, review pages 271-273.*

UNSCRAMBLE THE WORDS

116. **RONNESU**

□□□□□□◯

117. **APSYENS**

□◯□□◯◯□

118. **CIATUNOMO**

□□◯□□□◯◯□

119. **SHTOMO ULMSEC**

□□□□◯◯ □□□◯□◯

Take the circled letters, unscramble them, and fill in the solution.

What the man hoped the IRS agent would be during his audit.

120. □□□□□□□□□□□□□

APPLYING WHAT YOU KNOW

121. Mr. Hemstreet suffered a cerebrovascular accident, and it was determined that the resulting damage affected the left side of his cerebrum. On which side of his body will he most likely notice any paralysis?

122. Baby Dania was born with an excessive accumulation of cerebrospinal fluid in the ventricles. A catheter was placed in the ventricle and the fluid was drained by means of a shunt into the circulatory bloodstream. What condition does this medical history describe?

123. Mrs. Muhlenkamp looked out her window to see a man trapped under the wheel of a car. Although slightly built, Mrs. Muhlenkamp rushed to the car, lifted it, and saved the man. What division of the autonomic nervous system made this seemingly impossible task possible?

124. Lynn's heart raced and her palms became clammy as she watched the monster at the local theater. When the movie was over, however, she told her friends that she was not afraid at all. She appeared to be as calm as before the movie. What division of the autonomic nervous system made this possible?

125. Bill is scheduled to meet with his boss for his annual evaluation. He is planning to ask for a raise and hopes the evaluation will be good. Which subdivision of the autonomic nervous system will be active during this conference? Should he have a large meal before his appointment? Support your answer with facts from the chapter.

126. Word Find

Find and circle 14 terms presented in this chapter. Words may be spelled top to bottom, bottom to top, right to left, left to right, or diagonally.

Axon
Catecholamines
Dopamine
Endorphins
Ganglion
Glia
Microglia

Myelin
Oligodendroglia
Receptors
Serotonin
Synapse
Synaptic cleft
Tract

```
M  C  C  D  Q  S  Y  N  A  P  S  E  Q  G  O
E  N  A  Q  D  W  H  N  W  E  J  N  A  L  W
S  R  O  T  P  E  C  E  R  Y  Z  N  I  S  M
I  D  S  X  E  K  N  O  K  X  G  G  C  Y  Y
J  O  T  R  A  C  T  D  F  L  O  N  E  N  A
R  P  W  E  K  O  H  X  I  D  A  L  H  A  M
F  A  L  O  N  A  Y  O  E  I  I  I  X  P  C
C  M  Z  I  F  D  N  N  L  N  G  Z  U  T  Z
S  I  N  V  C  G  D  G  Z  A  N  A  K  I  P
G  N  A  T  Z  R  O  W  V  A  M  Y  T  C  O
K  E  N  D  O  R  P  H  I  N  S  I  L  C  X
C  P  Q  G  C  J  X  F  J  D  Q  S  N  L  F
X  U  L  I  H  I  G  Q  A  N  S  W  O  E  U
A  I  M  H  Q  E  X  K  D  B  W  Y  T  F  S
A  A  D  A  X  O  C  K  G  B  F  H  B  T  K
```

KNOW YOUR MEDICAL TERMS

True or False. Indicate in the blank space if the literal translation is true or false for the medical term.

_____ 127. astrocyte   star shaped/cell

_____ 128. axon   pole

_____ 129. efferent   away/carry/relating to

_____ 130. glia   glue

_____ 131. myelin   yellow/relating to

_____ 132. reflex arc   back/bend/curve

_____ 133. synapse   same/join/current

_____ 134. corpus callosum   body/callous

_____ 135. plexus   braid or network

▷ *If you had difficulty with this section, review pages 240 and 241.*

DID YOU KNOW?

- Although all pain is felt and interpreted in the brain, the brain itself has no pain sensation—even when cut!
- Your brain is more active when you sleep than during the day.
- The smarter you are, the more you dream. Some people even believe that they are smarter in their dreams than when they are awake.
- The brain has huge oxygen needs. It requires 20% of the oxygen and calories that your body needs—even though it only makes up 2% of your total body weight.

CHAPTER 11

The Senses

Consider this scene for a moment. You are walking along a beautiful beach while watching the sunset. You notice the various hues and are amazed at the multitude of shades that cover the sky. The waves are melodious as they splash along the shore, and you wiggle your feet with delight as you sense the warm, soft sand trickling between your toes. You sip on a soda and then inhale the fresh salt air as you continue your stroll along the shore. It is a memorable scene, but one that would not be possible without the assistance of your sense organs. The sense organs pick up messages that are sent over nerve pathways to specialized areas in the brain for interpretation. They make communication with and enjoyment of the environment possible. The visual, auditory, tactile, olfactory, and gustatory sense organs not only protect us from danger but also add an important dimension to our daily pleasures of life.

Your study of this chapter will give you an understanding of another one of the systems necessary for homeostasis and survival.

TOPICS FOR REVIEW

Before progressing to Chapter 12, you should review the classification of sense organs and the process for converting a stimulus into a sensation. Your study should also include an understanding of the special sense organs and the general sense organs.

CLASSIFICATION OF SENSE ORGANS

CONVERTING A STIMULUS INTO A SENSATION

GENERAL SENSE ORGANS

Match each term on the left with the corresponding description on the right.

_____ 1. Special sense organ   A. Olfactory cells

_____ 2. General sense organ   B. Detects stimuli such as pain or touch

_____ 3. Nose   C. Gustatory cells

_____ 4. Bulboid (Krause) corpuscle   D. Eye

_____ 5. Taste   E. Touch and possibly cold

▶ *If you had difficulty with this section, review pages 280-285 and Tables 11-1 and 11-2.*

SPECIAL SENSE ORGANS

Eye

Circle the correct answer.

6. The "white" of the eye is more commonly called the:
   A. Choroid
   B. Cornea
   C. Sclera
   D. Retina
   E. None of the above is correct.

7. The "colored" part of the eye is known as the:
   A. Retina
   B. Cornea
   C. Pupil
   D. Sclera
   E. Iris

8. The transparent portion of the sclera, referred to as the "window" of the eye, is the:
   A. Retina
   B. Cornea
   C. Pupil
   D. Iris

9. The mucous membrane that covers the front of the eye is called the:
   A. Cornea
   B. Choroid
   C. Conjunctiva
   D. Ciliary body
   E. None of the above is correct.

10. The structure that can contract or dilate to allow more or less light to enter the eye is the:
    A. Lens
    B. Choroid
    C. Retina
    D. Cornea
    E. Iris

11. When the eye is looking at objects far in the distance, the lens is _____ and the ciliary muscle is _____.
    A. Rounded, contracted
    B. Rounded, relaxed
    C. Slightly rounded, contracted
    D. Slightly curved, relaxed
    E. None of the above is correct

12. The lens of the eye is held in place by the:
    A. Ciliary muscle
    B. Aqueous humor
    C. Vitreous body
    D. Cornea

13. When the lens loses its elasticity and can no longer bring near objects into focus, the condition is known as:
    A. Glaucoma
    B. Presbyopia
    C. Astigmatism
    D. Strabismus

14. The fluid in front of the lens that is constantly being formed, drained, and replaced in the anterior cavity is the:
    A. Vitreous body
    B. Protoplasm
    C. Aqueous humor
    D. Conjunctiva

15. If drainage of the aqueous humor is blocked, the internal pressure within the eye will increase and a condition known as _____ could occur.
    A. Presbyopia
    B. Glaucoma
    C. Color blindness
    D. Cataracts

16. The rods and cones are the visual receptors and are located on the:
    A. Sclera
    B. Cornea
    C. Choroid
    D. Retina

17. Photoreception is the sense of:
    A. Vision
    B. Smell
    C. Taste
    D. Balance

18. The "blind spot" may also be referred to as the:
    A. Fovea centralis
    B. Macula lutea
    C. Retinal artery
    D. Optic disc

▶ *If you had difficulty with this section, review pages 285-289.*

UNSCRAMBLE THE WORDS

58. C A L R I E U

[ ][○][ ][ ][ ][ ]

59. R A E C L S

[○][ ][○][ ][ ][ ]

60. L A P I L A E P

[○][ ][○][ ][ ][ ][ ][ ]

61. C T V N U C N O I A J

[ ][ ][ ][ ][ ][ ][ ][ ][○][ ][ ]

Take the circled letters, unscramble them, and fill in the solution.

What Mr. Tuttle liked best about his classroom.

62. [ ][ ][ ][ ][ ][ ][ ]

APPLYING WHAT YOU KNOW

63. Mr. Nay was an avid swimmer and competed regularly in his age group. He had to withdraw from the last competition because of an infection of his ear. Antibiotics and analgesics were prescribed by the doctor. What is the medical term for his condition?

64. Mrs. Metheny loved the out-of-doors and spent a great deal of her spare time basking in the sun on the beach. Her physician suggested that she begin wearing sunglasses regularly when he noticed milky spots beginning to appear on Mrs. Metheny's lenses. What condition was Mrs. Metheny's physician trying to prevent from occurring?

65. Amanda repeatedly became ill with throat infections during her first few years of school. Lately, however, she has noticed that whenever she has a throat infection, her ears become very sore also. What might be the cause of this additional problem?

66. Richard was hit in the nose with a baseball during practice. His sense of smell was temporarily gone. What nerve receptors were damaged during the injury?

67. Word Find

Find and circle 19 terms presented in this chapter. Words may be spelled top to bottom, bottom to top, right to left, left to right, or diagonally.

Cataracts
Cerumen
Cochlea
Cones
Conjunctiva
Eustachian
Eye
Gustatory
Hyperopia
Incus

Mechanoreceptor
Olfactory
Papillae
Photopigment
Presbyopia
Receptors
Refraction
Rods
Senses

```
M  E  C  H  A  N  O  R  E  C  E  P  T  O  R
H  R  A  T  B  Q  I  R  T  B  N  H  M  A  E
P  F  T  Y  R  O  T  C  A  F  L  O  X  R  C
G  U  A  Y  I  N  A  I  H  C  A  T  S  U  E
G  P  R  A  C  E  R  U  M  E  N  O  P  X  P
I  E  A  I  P  O  Y  B  S  E  R  P  K  D  T
W  L  C  P  L  Y  N  E  Y  K  E  I  T  O  O
C  Q  T  O  I  B  R  J  B  S  F  G  L  M  R
Z  U  S  R  C  L  E  O  U  J  R  M  N  N  S
F  D  M  E  O  H  L  Q  T  N  A  E  Y  I  S
H  I  D  P  N  D  L  A  M  A  C  N  X  S  Z
A  M  L  Y  E  S  S  E  E  D  T  T  M  Z  H
D  D  M  H  S  F  E  X  A  Y  I  S  I  I  A
J  C  G  N  J  T  I  S  L  P  O  G  U  V  J
P  H  G  Y  A  K  H  S  U  C  N  I  S  G  A
```

KNOW YOUR MEDICAL TERMS

Use the following terms to construct medical terms from the given literal definitions.

chor   chemo   ulla
os   vestibule   on
gangli   crista   iris
aris   lymph   recept
endo   or   icle
ampu   oid   stapes

68. skin/like _____

69. within/water _____

70. know/unit _____

71. chemical/receive/agent _____

72. ridge/flask/little/relating to _____

73. rainbow _____

74. bone/little _____

75. stirrup _____

76. entrance hall _____

▶ *If you had difficulty with this section, review page 282.*

EYE

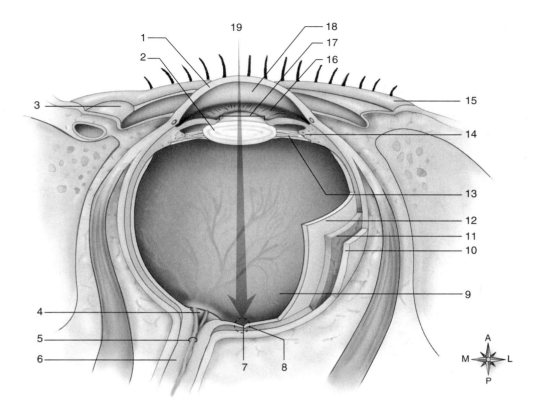

1. _____

2. _____

3. _____

4. _____

5. _____

6. _____

7. _____

8. _____

9. _____

10. _____

11. _____

12. _____

13. _____

14. _____

15. _____

16. _____

17. _____

18. _____

19. _____

EAR

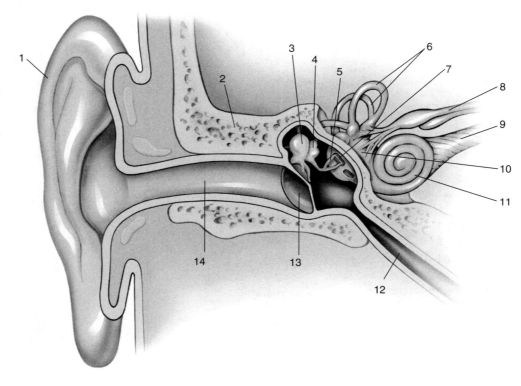

1. _____
2. _____
3. _____
4. _____
5. _____
6. _____
7. _____

8. _____
9. _____
10. _____
11. _____
12. _____
13. _____
14. _____

3. Which of the following statements is true regarding a young child whose growth is stunted, metabolism is low, sexual development is delayed, and mental development is retarded?
   A. The child suffers from cretinism.
   B. The child has an underactive thyroid.
   C. The child could suffer from a pituitary disorder.
   D. All of the above are true.

4. What can result when too much growth hormone is produced by the pituitary gland?
   A. Hyperglycemia
   B. A pituitary giant
   C. Both A and B
   D. None of the above

5. Which of the following glands is *not* regulated by the pituitary?
   A. Thyroid
   B. Ovaries
   C. Adrenals
   D. Thymus

6. Which of the following statements about the antidiuretic hormone is true?
   A. It is released by the posterior lobe of the pituitary.
   B. It causes diabetes insipidus when produced in insufficient amounts.
   C. It decreases urine volume.
   D. All of the above are true.

7. What controls the development of the body's immune system?
   A. Pituitary
   B. Thymus
   C. Pineal body
   D. Thyroid

8. Administration of what would best treat a person suffering from severe allergies?
   A. Gonadocorticoids
   B. Glucagon
   C. Mineralocorticoids
   D. Glucocorticoids

9. What endocrine gland is composed of cell clusters called the *islets of Langerhans*?
   A. Adrenals
   B. Thyroid
   C. Pituitary
   D. Pancreas

10. Which of the following statements concerning prostaglandins is true?
    A. They control activities of widely separated organs.
    B. They can be called *tissue hormones*.
    C. They diffuse over long distances to act on cells.
    D. All of the above are true.

Matching

Match each term in column A with the corresponding hormone in column B. (Only one answer is correct for each.)

Column A
_____ 11. Goiter
_____ 12. Ovulation
_____ 13. Diabetes mellitus
_____ 14. Lactation
_____ 15. Diabetes insipidus
_____ 16. Chorionic gonadotropins
_____ 17. Cushing syndrome
_____ 18. Labor
_____ 19. Acromegaly
_____ 20. Hypercalcemia

Column B
A. Glucocorticoid hormones
B. Antidiuretic hormone
C. Calcitonin
D. Oxytocin
E. Growth hormone
F. Placenta
G. Luteinizing hormone
H. Insulin
I. Prolactin
J. Thyroid hormones

ENDOCRINE GLANDS

1. _____

2. _____

3. _____

4. _____

5. _____

6. _____

7. _____

8. _____

9. _____

10. _____

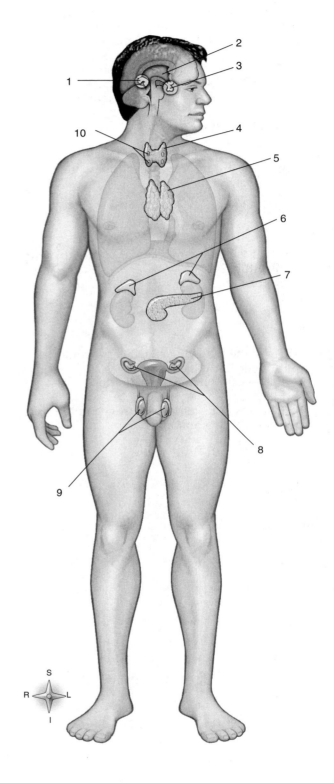

CHAPTER 13

Blood

Blood, the river of life, is the body's primary means of internal transportation. Although it is the respiratory system that provides oxygen for the body, the digestive system that provides nutrients, and the urinary system that eliminates wastes, none of these functions could be provided for the individual cells without blood. In less than 1 minute, a drop of blood will complete a trip through the entire body, distributing nutrients and collecting the wastes of metabolism.

Blood is divided into plasma (the liquid portion of blood) and the formed elements (the blood cells). There are three types of blood cells: red blood cells, white blood cells, and platelets. Together these cells and plasma provide a means of transportation that delivers the body's daily necessities.

Although all of us have red blood cells that are similar in shape, we have different blood types. Blood types are identified by the presence of certain antigens on the surface of red blood cells. Every person's blood belongs to one of four main blood groups: Type A, B, AB, or O. Any one of the four groups or "types" may or may not have the Rh factor present on the red blood cells. If an individual has a specific antigen called the Rh factor present on his or her blood, the blood is Rh positive. If this factor is missing, the blood is Rh negative. Approximately 85% of the population has the Rh factor (Rh positive), whereas 15% do not have the Rh factor (Rh negative).

Your understanding of this chapter will be necessary to prepare a proper foundation for learning about the circulatory system.

TOPICS FOR REVIEW

Before progressing to Chapter 14, you should have an understanding of the structure and function of blood plasma and cells. Your review should also include an understanding of blood types and Rh factors.

BLOOD COMPOSITION

MECHANISMS OF BLOOD DISEASE

Circle the correct answer.

1. Which one of the following substances is *not* a part of the plasma?
   A. Water
   B. Proteins
   C. Nutrients
   D. Waste products
   E. Leukocytes

2. The normal volume of blood in an adult is approximately:
   A. 2 to 3 pints
   B. 2 to 3 quarts
   C. 2 to 3 gallons
   D. 4 to 6 liters

3. Blood is normally:
   A. Very acidic
   B. Slightly acidic
   C. Neutral
   D. Slightly alkaline

4. Which is *not* a formed element?
   A. Leukocytes
   B. Erythrocytes
   C. Globulins
   D. Platelets

5. The liquid (extracellular) part of blood is the:
   A. Monocytes
   B. Plasma
   C. Basophils
   D. Lymphocytes

6. Myeloid tissue is _____ tissue.
   A. Epithelial
   B. Connective
   C. Muscle
   D. Nervous

7. A platelet may also be referred to as a/an:
   A. Neutrophil
   B. Eosinophil
   C. Thrombocyte
   D. Erythrocyte

8. An example of an agranular leukocyte is a/an:
   A. Platelet
   B. Erythrocyte
   C. Eosinophil
   D. Monocyte

9. Myeloid tissue is found in all of the following locations *except:*
   A. Sternum
   B. Ribs
   C. Wrist bones
   D. Hip bones
   E. Cranial bones

10. Lymphatic tissue is found in which of the following locations?
    A. Lymph nodes
    B. Thymus
    C. Spleen
    D. All of the above contain lymphatic tissue

11. If bone marrow failure is suspected, a procedure that allows for examination of the tissue is a/an:
    A. Aspiration biopsy cytology procedure
    B. Transplantation
    C. Stem cell smear
    D. Hematopoietic injection technique

12. The failure of blood-producing tissues to form blood cells properly may be due to:
    A. Radiation
    B. Inherited defects
    C. Viral infections
    D. All of the above

RED BLOOD CELLS

13. A red blood cell has:
    A. A biconcave disk shape that provides greater surface area for the exchange of dissolved gases and solutes.
    B. A large nucleus for rapid reproduction
    C. A life span of 6 months
    D. Several cytoplasmic organelles that maintain the homeostasis of the cell

14. The "buffy coat" layer that appears in the hematocrit tube contains:
    A. Red blood cells and platelets
    B. Plasma only
    C. Platelets only
    D. White blood cells and platelets
    E. None of the above is correct.

15. Any additional intracellular space that becomes available in a red blood cell is filled with:
    A. Iron
    B. Nutrients
    C. Hemoglobin
    D. ATP

16. The hematocrit value for red blood cells is _____ %.
    A. 75
    B. 60
    C. 50
    D. 45
    E. 35

17. A critical component of hemoglobin is:
    A. Potassium
    B. Calcium
    C. Vitamin K
    D. Iron

18. One of the most useful and frequently performed clinical blood tests is called the:
    A. WBC
    B. CBC
    C. RBC
    D. Hematocrit

 If you had difficulty with this section, review pages 336-345.

BLOOD TYPES

Rh SYSTEM

19. Fill in the blank areas.

BLOOD TYPE	ANTIGEN PRESENT IN RBC	ANTIBODY PRESENT IN PLASMA
A		Anti-B
B	B	
AB		None
O	None	

Fill in the blanks.

20. An _____ is a substance that can stimulate the body to make antibodies.

21. An _____ is a substance made by the body in response to stimulation by an antigen.

22. Many antibodies react with their antigens to clump or _____ them.

23. If a baby is born to an Rh-negative mother and Rh-positive father, it may develop the disease

_____ _____.

24. The term "Rh" is used because the antigen was first discovered in the blood of a

_____ _____.

25. The universal donor blood is _____.

26. The universal recipient blood is _____.

▷ *If you had difficulty with this section, review pages 345-348.*

RED BLOOD CELL DISORDERS

Matching

Match each term in column A with the corresponding description in column B.

27. _____ Pernicious anemia
28. _____ Polycythemia
29. _____ Sickle cell anemia
30. _____ Aplastic anemia
31. _____ Hemolytic anemia
32. _____ Thalassemia
33. _____ Erythroblastosis fetalis
34. _____ Iron-deficiency anemia
35. _____ Anemia

A. Dramatic increase in red blood cell numbers
B. Rh factor incompatibility
C. Production of abnormal type of hemoglobin
D. Low oxygen-carrying capacity of the blood
E. Decreased red blood cell life span
F. Lack of vitamin B_{12}
G. Abnormally low red blood cells and destruction of bone marrow
H. Ferrous sulfate is often used to treat this disorder
I. Inherited hemolytic anemia

▷ *If you had difficulty with this section, review pages 348-351.*

WHITE BLOOD CELLS

Multiple Choice

Circle the correct answer.

36. Another name for white blood cells is:
    A. Erythrocytes
    B. Leukocytes
    C. Thrombocytes
    D. Platelets

37. Which one of the following types of cells is *not* a granular leukocyte?
    A. Neutrophil
    B. Monocyte
    C. Basophil
    D. Eosinophil

38. An unusually low white blood cell count would be termed:
    A. Leukemia
    B. Leukopenia
    C. Leukocytosis
    D. Anemia
    E. None of the above is correct.

39. The most numerous of the phagocytes are the _____.
    A. Lymphocytes
    B. Neutrophils
    C. Basophils
    D. Eosinophils
    E. Monocytes

40. Which one of the following types of cells is *not* phagocytic?
    A. Neutrophils
    B. Eosinophils
    C. Lymphocytes
    D. Monocytes
    E. All of the above are phagocytic cells.

41. Which of the following cell types functions in the immune process?
    A. Neutrophils
    B. Lymphocytes
    C. Monocytes
    D. Basophils
    E. Reticuloendothelial cells

42. A special type of white blood cell count used as a diagnostic tool is known as a/an:
    A. Leukopenia
    B. Granulocyte count
    C. Differential WBC count
    D. CBC

 If you had difficulty with this section, review pages 351-353.

WHITE BLOOD CELL DISORDERS

Matching

Match each term in column A with the corresponding description in column B.

Column A

43. _____ Multiple myeloma
44. _____ Leukemia
45. _____ Acute lymphocytic leukemia
46. _____ Chronic myeloid leukemia
47. _____ Acute myeloid leukemia
48. _____ Infectious mononucleosis
49. _____ Lymphoid neoplasms
50. _____ Chronic lymphocytic leukemia

Column B

A. Most common form of blood cancer in children between 3 to 7 years of age

B. Results from cancerous transformation of granulocytic precursor cells in the bone marrow

C. Most common blood cancer in people over 65 years of age

D. Arises from lymphoid precursor cells that normally produce B lymphocytes, T lymphocytes, or their descendant cell types

E. General classification for a number of blood cancers affecting white blood cells

F. Malignant precursor B lymphocytes are produced in large numbers.

G. Usually caused by the Epstein-Barr virus (EBV)

H. Prognosis is poor with only 50% of children and 30% of adults achieving long-term survival.

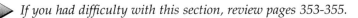 *If you had difficulty with this section, review pages 353-355.*

PLATELETS

BLOOD CLOTTING

BLOOD CLOTTING DISORDERS

Circle the correct answer.

51. Vitamin K stimulates liver cells to increase the synthesis of:
    A. Prothrombin
    B. Thrombin
    C. Platelets
    D. Heparin
    E. Calcium

52. Thrombocytes:
    A. Are tiny cell fragments
    B. Are filled with chemicals necessary to initiate blood clotting
    C. Are formed elements
    D. All of the above

53. If part of a clot dislodges and circulates through the bloodstream, the dislodged part is called a/an:
    A. Thrombus
    B. Thrombosis
    C. Anticoagulant
    D. Clotting factor
    E. Embolus

54. Which of the following is *not* a critical component of coagulation?
    A. Thrombin
    B. Fibrinolysis
    C. Fibrinogen
    D. Fibrin

55. Which of the following does *not* hasten clotting?
    A. A rough spot in the endothelium
    B. Abnormally slow blood flow
    C. Heparin
    D. All of the above hasten clotting.

Circle the correct response.

56. Tissue plasminogen activator (TPA) is used to dissolve *(heart* or *hemorrhagic stroke)* clots.

57. An International Normalized Ratio (INR) of *(0.8* or *2.5)* is normal.

58. The disease that results from a failure to form blood clotting factor VIII is *(thrombocytopenia* or *hemophilia).*

59. Reduced platelet count is common in diseases such as *(thrombosis* or *HIV/AIDS).*

60. Hemophilia involves avoiding such common drugs as *(aspirin* or *antihistamines).*

▷ *If you had difficulty with this section, review pages 355-359.*

UNSCRAMBLE THE WORDS

61. **H G A P O Y C E T**

    ⬡ ☐ ☐ ☐ ⬡ ☐ ☐

62. **N T H I R B M O**

    ⬡ ☐ ☐ ☐ ☐ ☐ ⬡

63. **A T N I G N E**

    ☐ ☐ ☐ ⬡ ☐ ☐ ☐

64. **B R N I F I**

    ☐ ⬡ ☐ ☐ ☐ ☐

Take the circled letters, unscramble them, and fill in the solution.

What Shelley thought was the most difficult task to learn on her new computer.

65. ☐ ☐ ☐ ☐ ☐ ☐

APPLYING WHAT YOU KNOW

66. Mrs. Florez's blood type is O positive. Her husband's type is O negative. Her newborn baby's blood type is O negative. Is there any need for concern with this combination?

67. After Mrs. Freund's baby was born, the doctor applied a gauze dressing for a short time on the umbilical cord. He also gave the baby a dose of vitamin K. Why did the doctor perform these two procedures?

68. Valerie is a teenager with a picky appetite. She loves junk food and seldom eats properly. She complains of being tired all the time. A visit to her doctor reveals a hemoglobin of 10 and RBCs that are classified as hypochromic. What condition does Valerie have?

69. Jack was prescribed a daily dose of Coumadin since his diagnosis of atrial fibrillation. He was advised that he must be monitored monthly with a lab test to regulate his dosage. What is the name of that lab test? Describe how the test is performed and the information that it provides for the doctor.

70. Word Find

Find and circle 24 terms presented in this chapter. Words may be spelled top to bottom, bottom to top, right to left, left to right, or diagonally.

```
H  S  H  K  L  S  U  L  O  B  M  E  A  E  S
K  E  E  V  M  Z  H  E  P  A  R  I  N  D  N
D  T  M  F  A  C  T  O  R  Y  E  T  I  Q  P
O  Y  A  O  H  N  B  A  T  Q  Y  A  R  A  R
N  C  T  J  G  W  E  H  N  P  N  L  B  U  D
O  O  O  S  Q  L  R  M  E  T  I  S  I  P  M
R  K  C  E  M  O  O  N  I  H  I  Q  F  W  W
H  U  R  T  C  N  I  B  P  A  S  G  Z  T  G
E  E  I  Y  O  B  O  O  I  V  E  W  E  T  X
S  L  T  C  M  D  S  E  C  N  R  T  U  N  R
U  E  Y  O  Y  A  I  M  E  K  U  E  L  Y  S
S  T  R  G  B  S  T  H  R  O  M  B  U  S  Q
E  H  Z  A  M  S  A  L  P  N  D  Z  P  O  N
T  E  N  H  F  P  D  A  P  M  E  E  I  B  W
E  W  B  P  H  K  B  O  N  C  K  W  X  V  J
```

AIDS	Factor	Phagocytes
Anemia	Fibrin	Plasma
Antibody	Hematocrit	Recipient
Antigen	Hemoglobin	Rhesus
Basophil	Heparin	Serum
Donor	Leukemia	Thrombin
Embolus	Leukocytes	Thrombus
Erythrocytes	Monocyte	Type

KNOW YOUR MEDICAL TERMS

Select the literal translations for the medical terms.

71. _____ Leukocyte	A. red/cell
72. _____ Platelet	B. clot/substance
73. _____ Macrophage	C. neither/love
74. _____ Hematocrit	D. flat/small
75. _____ Heparin	E. white/cell
76. _____ Myeloma	F. blood/separate
77. _____ Neutrophil	G. large/eat
78. _____ Erythrocyte	H. marrow/tumor
79. _____ Purpura	I. liver/substance
80. _____ Thrombin	J. purple

▶ *If you had difficulty with this section, review pages 338 and 339.*

BLOOD

Fill in the crossword puzzle.

ACROSS

1. Abnormally high WBC count
4. Final stage of clotting process
6. Oxygen-carrying mechanism of blood
9. To engulf and digest microbes
10. Stationary blood clot
12. RBC
13. Circulating blood clot
14. Liquid portion of blood

DOWN

2. Type O (two words)
3. Substances that stimulate the body to make antibodies
5. Type of leukocyte
7. Platelets
8. Prevents clotting of blood
11. Inability of the blood to carry sufficient oxygen

DID YOU KNOW?

- Blood products are good for approximately 3 to 6 weeks, but fresh frozen plasma is good for at least 6 months.
- In the second it takes to turn the page of a book, you will lose about 3 million red blood cells. During that same second, your bone marrow will have produced the same number of new ones.
- There is enough iron in a human to make a small nail.
- Statistics show that 25% or more of us will require blood at least once in our lifetime.

CHECK YOUR KNOWLEDGE

Multiple Choice

Circle the correct answer.

1. Which of the following statements is false?
   A. Sickle cell anemia is caused by a genetic defect.
   B. Leukemia is characterized by a low number of WBCs.
   C. Polycythemia is characterized by an abnormally high number of erythrocytes.
   D. Pernicious anemia is caused by a lack of vitamin B_{12}.

2. Deficiency in the number or function of erythrocytes is called:
   A. Leukemia
   B. Anemia
   C. Polycythemia
   D. Leukopenia

3. Which of the following statements does *not* describe a characteristic of leukocytes?
   A. They are disk-shaped cells that do not contain a nucleus.
   B. They have the ability to fight infection.
   C. They provide defense against certain parasites.
   D. They provide immune defense.

4. Red bone marrow forms all of the following blood cells *except:*
   A. Platelets and basophils
   B. Lymphocytes
   C. Red blood cells
   D. Neutrophils and eosinophils

5. Which of the following substances is *not* found in blood plasma?
   A. Albumins
   B. Gases
   C. Waste products
   D. All of the above substances are found in blood plasma.

6. An allergic reaction may increase the number of:
   A. Eosinophils
   B. Neutrophils
   C. Lymphocytes
   D. Monocytes

7. What is a blood clot that is moving through the body called?
   A. Embolism
   B. Fibrosis
   C. Heparin
   D. Thrombosis

8. When could difficulty with the Rh blood factor arise?
   A. When an Rh-negative man and woman produce a child.
   B. When an Rh-positive man and woman produce a child.
   C. When an Rh-positive woman and an Rh-negative man produce a child.
   D. When an Rh-negative woman and an Rh-positive man produce a child.

9. What is the primary function of hemoglobin?
   A. To fight infection
   B. To make blood clots
   C. To carry oxygen
   D. To transport hormones

10. Which of the following steps are *not* involved in blood clot formation?
    A. A blood vessel is injured and platelet factors are formed.
    B. Thrombin is converted into prothrombin.
    C. Fibrinogen is converted into fibrin.
    D. All of the above are involved in blood clot formation.

Matching

Match each term in column A with its corresponding term or description in column B. (Only one answer is correct for each.)

Column A

_____ 11. Lymphocytes

_____ 12. Erythrocytes

_____ 13. Type AB

_____ 14. Basophils

_____ 15. Leukemia

_____ 16. Platelets

_____ 17. Type O

_____ 18. Rh factor

_____ 19. Red bone marrow

_____ 20. Neutrophils

Column B

A. Heparin

B. Contains anti-A and anti-B antibodies

C. Clotting

D. Immunity

E. Erythroblastosis fetalis

F. Anemia

G. Cancer

H. Contains A and B antigens

I. Myeloid tissue

J. Phagocytosis

MATCHING

Match each numbered descriptive term with the related formed element and write the corresponding letter in the answer blank.

A. Red blood cells   B. White blood cells   C. Platelets

21. _____ Rh factor

22. _____ Agranulocytes

23. _____ Macrophages

24. _____ Thrombocytes

25. _____ Hemophilia

26. _____ Prothrombin time

27. _____ Hemoglobin

28. _____ Blood types

29. _____ Hematocrit

30. _____ Eosinophils

HUMAN BLOOD CELLS

Fill in the missing areas of the table.

BODY CELL		FUNCTION

BLOOD TYPING

Using the key below the table shown, draw the appropriate reaction with the donor's blood in the circles provided.

Recipient's blood		Reactions with donor's blood			
RBC antigens	Plasma antibodies	Donor type O	Donor type A	Donor type B	Donor type AB
None (Type O)	Anti-A Anti-B	◯	◯	◯	◯
A (Type A)	Anti-B	◯	◯	◯	◯
B (Type B)	Anti-A	◯	◯	◯	◯
AB (Type AB)	(None)	◯	◯	◯	◯

 Normal blood    Agglutinated blood

CHAPTER 14

The Heart

The heart is actually two pumps—one moves blood to the lungs, the other pushes it out into the body. These two functions seem rather elementary in comparison to the complex and numerous functions performed by most of the other body organs, and yet if this pump stops, within a few short minutes all life ceases.

The heart is divided into two upper compartments called *atria,* or receiving chambers, and two lower compartments, or discharging chambers, called *ventricles*. By age 45, approximately 300,000 tons of blood will have passed through these chambers to be circulated to the blood vessels. This closed system of circulation provides distribution of blood to the entire body (systemic circulation) and to specific regions, such as the pulmonary circulation or coronary circulation.

The beating of the heart must be coordinated in a rhythmic manner if the heart is to pump effectively. This is achieved by electrical impulses that are stimulated by specialized structures embedded in the walls of the heart. The sinoatrial node, atrioventricular node, bundle of His, and Purkinje fibers combine efforts to conduct the tiny electrical currents necessary to contract the heart. Any interruption or failure of this system may result in serious pathology or death.

A healthy heart is necessary to pump sufficient blood throughout the body to nourish and oxygenate cells continuously. Your review of this chapter will provide you with an understanding of this vital organ that is necessary for survival.

TOPICS FOR REVIEW

Before progressing to Chapter 15, you should have an understanding of the structure and function of the heart. Your review should include a study of the coronary circulation and the conduction system of the heart. Your study should conclude with an understanding of the major coronary diseases and disorders.

ANATOMY OF THE HEART

HEART VALVES AND VALVE DISORDERS

Fill in the blanks.

1. The system that supplies our cells' transportation needs is the

   _____ _____.

2. The _____ or blunt point at the lower edge of the heart lies on the diaphragm, pointing to the left.

3. The _____ _____ divides the heart into right and left sides between the atria.

4. The _____ are the two upper chambers of the heart.

5. The _____ are the two lower chambers of the heart.

6. The cardiac muscle tissue is referred to as the _____.

7. Inflammation of the heart lining is _____.

8. The two AV valves are _____ and _____.

9. The inner layer of the pericardium is called the _____

   _____ or _____.

10. The outer layer of pericardium is called _____

    _____.

11. If the pericardium becomes inflamed, a condition called _____ results.

12. The _____ _____ are located between the two
    ventricular chambers and the large arteries that carry blood away from the heart when contraction occurs.

13. A _____ _____

    _____ is a condition caused when the flaps of this valve extend back into
    the left atrium, causing the valve to leak.

14. _____ _____ _____
    is cardiac damage resulting from a delayed inflammatory response to a streptococcal infection that occurs
    most often in children.

▶ *If you had difficulty with this section, review pages 367-373.*

HEART SOUNDS

BLOOD FLOW THROUGH THE HEART

CORONARY CIRCULATION AND CORONARY HEART DISEASE

Select the term that best matches each of the numbered descriptions. Write the corresponding letter in the answer blank.

_____ 15. Movement of blood from the left
            ventricle through the body

_____ 16. Blood clot

_____ 17. Myocardial infarction

_____ 18. Abnormal heart sound often caused by
            disorders of the valves

_____ 19. Movement of blood from the right
            ventricle to the lungs

_____ 20. Hardening of the arteries

_____ 21. Severe chest pain

_____ 22. High blood pressure

_____ 23. Structures through which blood returns
            to the left atrium

_____ 24. Treatment for certain coronary disorders

A. Heart murmur
B. Pulmonary circulation
C. Embolism
D. Heart attack
E. Angina pectoris
F. Systemic circulation
G. Atherosclerosis
H. Hypertension
I. Coronary bypass
J. Pulmonary veins

▶ *If you had difficulty with this section, review pages 373-377.*

CARDIAC CYCLE AND THE CONDUCTION SYSTEM OF THE HEART

CARDIAC DYSRHYTHMIAS

CARDIAC OUTPUT

HEART FAILURE

Circle the correct answer.

25. The heart beats at an average rate of
_____ beats per minute.
A. 50
B. 72
C. 100
D. 120

26. Each complete beat of the heart is called:
A. Cardiac output
B. Stroke volume
C. A cardiac cycle
D. A contraction

27. The pacemaker of the heart is also known as the:
A. SA node
B. AV node
C. AV bundle
D. Purkinje fibers

28. A rapid heart rhythm, over 100 beats per minutes, is referred to as:
A. Bradycardia
B. Sinus arrhythmia
C. Tachycardia
D. Premature contractions

29. The term _____ describes the electrical activity that triggers contraction of the heart muscle.
A. Depolarization
B. Repolarization
C. AV node block
D. Cardiac arrhythmia

30. A diagnostic tool that uses ultrasound to detect valve and heart disorders is known as a/an:
A. Electrocardiogram
B. Pacemaker
C. TPA
D. Echocardiogram

31. Frequent premature contractions can lead to:
A. Extra systoles
B. Bradycardia
C. Fibrillation
D. Heart failure

32. A drug that slows and increases the strength of cardiac contractions is:
A. Digitalis
B. Nitroglycerin
C. Calcium-channel blocker
D. Anticoagulant

33. Congestive heart failure inevitably causes:
A. Extra systole
B. Pulmonary edema
C. Fibrillation
D. Bradycardia

34. Failure of the right side of the heart due to blockage of pulmonary blood flow is called:
A. Cardiomyopathy
B. Ventricular fibrillation
C. Cor pulmonale
D. TPA

35. A nonmedical rescuer can defibrillate a victim in ventricular fibrillation with the use of a/an:
A. AED
B. Beta blocker
C. Demand pacemaker
D. ECG

36. Coumadin and dicumarol are examples of commonly used oral:
A. Beta blockers
B. Nitroglycerines
C. Calcium-channel blockers
D. Anticoagulants

True or False

If the statement is true, write "T" in the answer blank. If the statement is false, correct the statement by circling the incorrect term(s) and writing the correct term(s) in the answer blank.

37. _____ Most of the atrial blood moves into the ventricles before the atria have a chance to contract.

38. _____ Cardiac muscle fibers are unable to contract rhythmically on their own.

39. _____ The four structures embedded in the wall of the heart that make up the conduction system of the heart are the SA node, the pacemaker, the AV bundle, and the bundle of His.

40. _____ A special type of radiography used to visualize arteries is known as angiography.

41. _____ The T wave on an ECG results from the electrical activity generated by repolarization of the ventricles.

42. _____ Heart block may be treated by implanting an artificial pacemaker.

43. _____ Atrial ablation treats atrial fibrillation by dilating the pathway of abnormal electrical signals.

44. _____ Cardiac output (CO) is the volume of blood pumped by one atrium per minute.

45. _____ The sympathetic division of the ANS decreases the heart rate.

46. _____ Stroke volume (SV) refers to the volume of blood ejected from the ventricles during each beat.

47. _____ Stroke volume may be decreased due to several causes such as ion imbalances, valve disorders, coronary artery blockages, or myocardial infarctions.

▷ *If you had difficulty with this section, review pages 377-385.*

UNSCRAMBLE THE WORDS

48. **C T S S Y M E I**

49. **L M T R I A**

50. **T H R E A**

51. **S B T U M H O R**

Take the circled letters, unscramble them, and fill in the solution.

What Tom lacked on the dance floor.

52.

APPLYING WHAT YOU KNOW

53. Else was experiencing angina pectoris. Her doctor suggests a surgical procedure that would require the removal of a vein from another region of her body, which would then be used to bypass a partial blockage in her coronary arteries. What is this procedure called?

54. Phil has a heart block. His electrical impulses are being blocked and prevented from reaching the ventricles. An electrical device that causes ventricular contractions at a rate necessary to maintain circulation is being considered as possible treatment for his condition. What is this device?

55. Mrs. Haygood was diagnosed with an acute case of endocarditis. What is the real danger of this diagnosis?

56. Jeanne's homework assignment was to demonstrate knowledge of the path of blood flow through the heart. Can you help her?

    Trace the blood flow through the heart by numbering the following structures in the correct sequence. Start with number 1, the vena cava, where blood enters the heart, and proceed until you have numbered all 12 structures.

    _____ Tricuspid valve   _____ Pulmonary veins
    _____ Pulmonary arteries   _____ Pulmonary semilunar valve
    _____ Bicuspid valve   _____ Left ventricle
    _____ Vena cava   _____ Right atrium
    _____ Right ventricle   _____ Left atrium
    _____ Aorta   _____ Aortic semilunar valve

57. Word Find

Find and circle 12 terms presented in this chapter. Words may be spelled top to bottom, bottom to top, right to left, left to right, or diagonally.

```
P  W  S  T  L  W  G  V  F  V  W  Q  U  S  Y
U  T  X  U  L  Q  L  V  M  J  W  O  U  J  D
R  E  S  P  E  B  S  W  Z  W  K  N  X  Q  Y
K  V  Y  T  E  V  E  N  T  R  I  C  L  E  S
I  F  K  U  O  E  L  O  T  S  Y  S  X  V  R
N  G  Z  O  A  R  G  A  Y  C  M  X  F  K  H
J  B  B  C  U  J  T  R  V  K  P  Y  P  W  Y
E  V  L  A  V  R  A  N  U  L  I  M  E  S  T
F  D  T  I  Z  N  H  I  Y  A  A  D  U  T  H
I  T  B  D  O  D  S  H  Y  P  U  R  W  I  M
B  P  E  R  I  C  A  R  D  I  U  M  T  D  I
E  M  O  A  B  R  A  D  Y  C  A  R  D  I  A
R  C  U  C  E  N  D  O  C  A  R  D  I  U  M
S  A  I  D  R  A  C  Y  H  C  A  T  B  Y  P
```

Bradycardia	Endocardium	Semilunar valve
Cardiac output	Mitral valve	Systole
Coronary sinus	Pericardium	Tachycardia
Dysrhythmia	Purkinje fibers	Ventricle

KNOW YOUR MEDICAL TERMS

Fill in the blank with the proper medical term.

58. entrance or courtyard _____

59. string or cord/pulled tight _____

60. contraction _____

61. strangling/breast/relating to _____

62. heart/muscle/disease/state _____

63. electricity/heart/drawing _____

64. within/heart/thing _____

65. slow/heart/condition _____

66. plug/condition _____

67. fiber/little/process _____

▶ *If you had difficulty with this section, review pages 368 and 369.*

DID YOU KNOW?

- Your heart pumps more than 5 quarts of blood every minute—that's 2000 gallons a day!
- People who have an optimistic attitude as opposed to a pessimistic attitude suffer few strokes and heart attacks and have a 55% less chance of suffering cardiovascular diseases.
- A kitchen faucet would need to be turned on all the way for at least 45 years to equal the amount of blood pumped by the heart in an average lifetime.
- German surgeon Werner Forssmann (1904-1979) examined the inside of his own heart in 1929 by threading a catheter into his arm vein and pushing it 20 inches into his heart, inventing cardiac catheterization—a now common procedure.

HEART AND HEART DISEASE

Fill in the crossword puzzle.

ACROSS

1. Inflammation of the pericardium
3. A condition in which muscle fibers contract out of step with each other
6. Disease of the myocardial tissue
8. Also known as the *visceral pericardium*
9. Relaxation of the heart
10. Upper chambers of the heart

DOWN

2. Heart specialist
4. Also known as the *sinoatrial node*
5. Complex that occurs as a result of depolarization of the ventricles
7. Also known as the *mitral valve*
8. Graphic record of the heart's electrical activity

CHECK YOUR KNOWLEDGE

Multiple Choice

Circle the correct answer.

1. The superior vena cava carries blood to the:
   A. Left ventricle
   B. Coronary arteries
   C. Right atrium
   D. Pulmonary veins

2. Which of the following events, if any, does *not* precede ventricular contraction?
   A. P wave
   B. Atrial depolarization
   C. Ventricular depolarization
   D. All of these events precede contraction.

3. Which of the following pairs is mismatched?
   A. Angina pectoris—chest pain
   B. Congestive heart failure—left-sided heart failure
   C. Tachycardia—slow heart rhythm
   D. Dysrhythmia—heart block

4. Which of the following statements is *not* true regarding pericarditis?
   A. It may be caused by infection or trauma.
   B. It often causes severe chest pain.
   C. It may result in impairment of the pumping action of the heart.
   D. All of the above statements are true.

5. The outside covering that surrounds and protects the heart is called the:
   A. Endocardium
   B. Myocardium
   C. Pericardium
   D. Ectocardium

6. Thin-walled upper heart cavities that receive blood from veins are called:
   A. Chordae tendineae
   B. Atria
   C. Pericardia
   D. Ventricles

7. A valve that permits blood to flow from the right ventricle into the pulmonary artery is called:
   A. Tricuspid
   B. Mitral
   C. Aortic semilunar
   D. Pulmonary semilunar

8. Ventricular contraction of the heart occurs *immediately after* depolarization of the:
   A. Purkinje fibers
   B. Atrioventricular node
   C. Sinoatrial node
   D. Bundle of His

9. A variation in heart rate during the breathing cycle is called:
   A. Mitral valve prolapse
   B. Fibrillation
   C. Sinus dysrhythmia
   D. None of the above

10. Heart implants:
    A. Allow patients to move around freely without external pumps
    B. Are artificial hearts that are made of biologically inert synthetic materials
    C. Still have limited use
    D. All of the above are true.

Matching

Match each term in column A with its corresponding term in column B. (Only one answer is correct for each.)

Column A

_____ 11. Heart attack

_____ 12. QRS complex

_____ 13. Systole

_____ 14. Pulmonary circulation

_____ 15. Bicuspid

_____ 16. Heart compression

_____ 17. Heart muscle

_____ 18. Pacemaker

_____ 19. T wave

_____ 20. Chest pain

Column B

A. Sinoatrial node

B. Cardiac tamponade

C. Myocardium

D. Ventricular repolarization

E. Angina pectoris

F. Myocardial infarction

G. Ventricular depolarization

H. Ventricular contraction

I. Lungs

J. Mitral

THE HEART

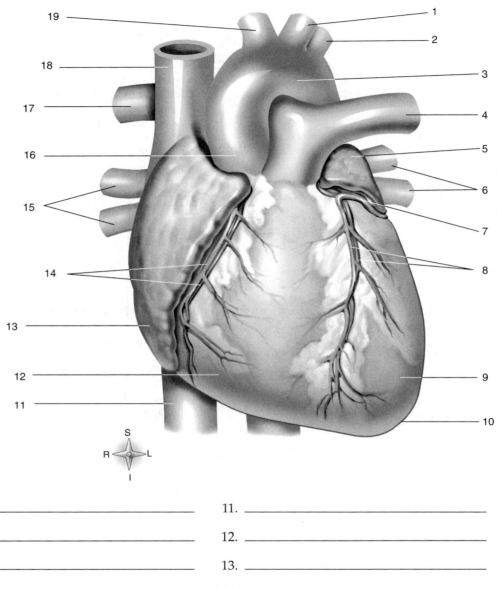

1. _____

2. _____

3. _____

4. _____

5. _____

6. _____

7. _____

8. _____

9. _____

10. _____

11. _____

12. _____

13. _____

14. _____

15. _____

16. _____

17. _____

18. _____

19. _____

CONDUCTION SYSTEM OF THE HEART

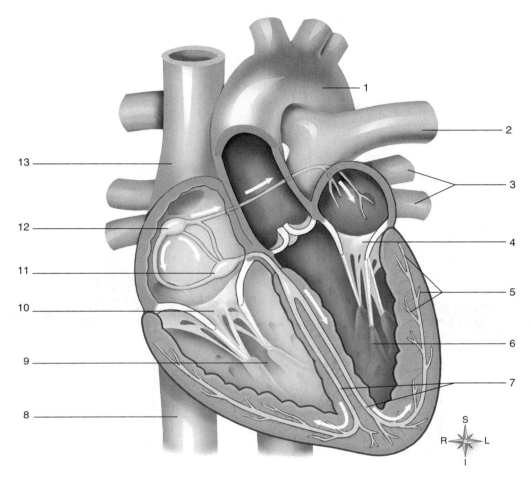

1. _____
2. _____
3. _____
4. _____
5. _____
6. _____
7. _____

8. _____
9. _____
10. _____
11. _____
12. _____
13. _____

NORMAL ECG DEFLECTIONS

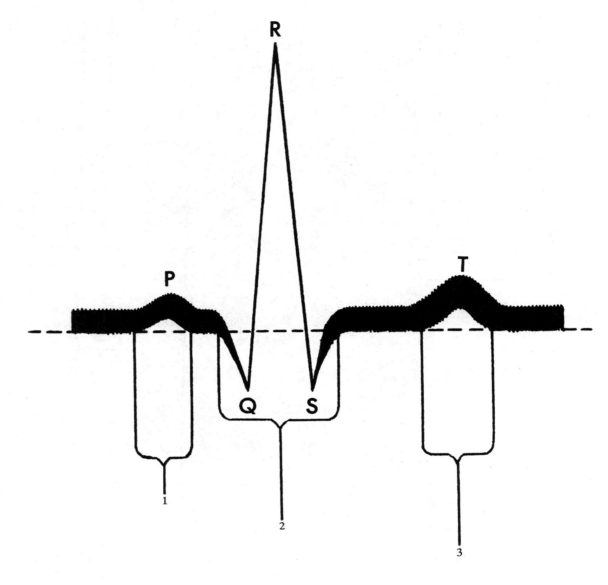

1. _____   3. _____

2. _____

CHAPTER 15

The Circulation of the Blood

One hundred thousand miles of blood vessels make up the elaborate transportation system that circulates materials needed for energy, growth and repair, and also eliminates wastes from your body. These vessels, called *arteries, veins*, and *capillaries*, serve different functions. Arteries carry blood from the heart, veins carry blood to the heart, and capillaries are exchange vessels, or connecting links, between the arteries and veins. The pumping action of the heart keeps blood moving, or circulating, through this closed system of vessels. This system provides distribution of blood to the entire body (systemic circulation) and to specific regions such as the pulmonary circulation or hepatic portal circulation.

Blood pressure is the force of blood in the vessels. This force is highest in the arteries and lowest in the veins. Normal blood pressure varies among individuals and depends on the volume of blood in the arteries. The larger the volume of blood in the arteries, the more pressure is exerted on the walls of the arteries, and the higher the arterial pressure. Conversely, the less blood in the arteries, the lower the blood pressure.

A functional cardiovascular system is vital for survival because without circulation, tissues would lack a supply of oxygen and nutrients. Waste products would begin to accumulate and could become toxic. Your review of this system will provide you with an understanding of the complex transportation mechanism of the body necessary for survival.

TOPICS FOR REVIEW

Before progressing to Chapter 16, you should have an understanding of the structure and function of the blood vessels. Your review should include a study of systemic, pulmonary, hepatic portal, and fetal circulation and should conclude with a thorough understanding of blood pressure, pulse, and circulatory shock.

BLOOD VESSELS

Match each term on the left with its corresponding description on the right.

_____ 1. Arteries

_____ 2. Veins

_____ 3. Capillaries

_____ 4. Tunica externa

_____ 5. Precapillary sphincters

_____ 6. Superior vena cava

_____ 7. Aorta

A. Smooth muscle cells that guard the entrance to capillaries

B. Carry blood to the heart

C. Function as exchange vessels

D. Carry blood away from the heart

E. Largest vein

F. Carries blood out of the left ventricle

G. Outermost layer of arteries and veins

▶ *If you had difficulty with this section, review pages 390-394.*

DISORDERS OF BLOOD VESSELS

Match each definition on the left with its corresponding term on the right.

_____ 8. Hardening of the arteries

_____ 9. Decreased blood supply to a tissue

_____ 10. Tissue death

_____ 11. Necrosis that has progressed to decay

_____ 12. A type of arteriosclerosis caused by lipids

_____ 13. A section of an artery that has become abnormally widened

_____ 14. Varicose veins in the rectum

_____ 15. Vein inflammation

_____ 16. Clot formation

_____ 17. Cerebral vascular accident

A. Atherosclerosis

B. Ischemia

C. Aneurysm

D. Necrosis

E. Gangrene

F. Hemorrhoids

G. Phlebitis

H. Stroke

I. Arteriosclerosis

J. Thrombus

▶ *If you had difficulty with this section, review pages 394-399.*

CIRCULATION OF BLOOD

Circle the correct answer.

18. The aorta carries blood out of the:
    A. Right atrium
    B. Left atrium
    C. Right ventricle
    D. Left ventricle
    E. None of the above

19. The superior vena cava returns blood to the:
    A. Left atrium
    B. Left ventricle
    C. Right atrium
    D. Right ventricle
    E. None of the above

20. The _____ function as exchange vessels.
    A. Venules
    B. Capillaries
    C. Arteries
    D. Arterioles
    E. Veins

21. Blood returns from the lungs during pulmonary circulation via the:
    A. Pulmonary artery
    B. Pulmonary veins
    C. Aorta
    D. Inferior vena cava

22. The hepatic portal circulation serves the body by:
    A. Removing excess glucose and storing it in the liver as glycogen
    B. Detoxifying blood
    C. Assisting the body to maintain proper blood glucose balance
    D. All of the above

23. The structure used to bypass the liver in the fetal circulation is the:
    A. Foramen ovale
    B. Ductus venosus
    C. Ductus arteriosus
    D. Umbilical vein

24. The foramen ovale serves the fetal circulation by:
    A. Connecting the aorta and the pulmonary artery
    B. Shunting blood from the right atrium directly into the left atrium
    C. Bypassing the liver
    D. Bypassing the lungs

25. The structure used to connect the aorta and pulmonary artery in the fetal circulation is the:
    A. Ductus arteriosus
    B. Ductus venosus
    C. Aorta
    D. Foramen ovale

26. Which of the following is *not* an artery?
    A. Femoral
    B. Popliteal
    C. Coronary
    D. Inferior vena cava

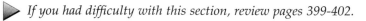 *If you had difficulty with this section, review pages 399-402.*

BLOOD PRESSURE

PULSE

True or False

If the statement is true, write "T" in the answer blank. If the statement is false, correct the statement by circling the incorrect term and writing the correct term in the answer blank.

_____ 27. Blood pressure is highest in the veins and lowest in the arteries.

_____ 28. The difference between two blood pressures is referred to as *blood pressure deficit*.

_____ 29. If the blood pressure in the arteries were to decrease so that it became equal to the average pressure in the arterioles, circulation would increase.

_____ 30. A stroke is often the result of low blood pressure.

_____ 31. Massive hemorrhage increases blood pressure.

_____ 32. Blood pressure is the volume of blood in the vessels.

_____ 33. Both the strength and the rate of heartbeat affect cardiac output and blood pressure.

_____ 34. The diameter of the arterioles helps determine how much blood drains out of arteries into arterioles.

_____ 35. A stronger heartbeat tends to decrease blood pressure and a weaker heartbeat tends to increase it.

_____ 36. The systolic pressure is the pressure being exerted against the vessels while the ventricles relax.

_____ 37. If blood becomes less viscous than normal, blood pressure increases.

_____ 38. A device called a *sphygmomanometer* is used to measure blood pressures in clinical situations.

_____ 39. Loud, tapping Korotkoff sounds suddenly begin when the cuff pressure measured by the mercury column equals the systolic pressure.

_____ 40. The venous blood pressure within the left atrium is called the *central venous pressure*.

_____ 41. The pulse is a vein expanding and then recoiling.

_____ 42. The radial artery is located at the wrist.

_____ 43. The common carotid artery is located in the neck along the front edge of the sternocleidomastoid muscle.

_____ 44. The artery located at the bend of the elbow that is used for locating the pulse is the dorsalis pedis.

▶ _If you had difficulty with this section, review pages 402-408._

CIRCULATORY SHOCK

Fill in the blanks.

45. Complications of septicemia may result in _____

_____.

46. _____ _____ results from any type of heart failure.

47. An acute type of allergic reaction called _____ results in

_____ _____.

48. _____ _____ results from wide-spread dilation of blood vessels caused by an imbalance in autonomic stimulation of smooth muscles in vessel walls.

49. _Hypovolemia_ means "_____ _____

_____."

50. A type of septic shock that results from staphylococcal infections that begin in the vagina of menstruating women and spread to the blood is _____

_____ _____.

▶ _If you had difficulty with this section, review pages 408-410._

UNSCRAMBLE THE WORDS

51. **S T M E S Y C I**

    ⬡ ⬡ ☐ ☐ ☐ ☐ ☐

52. **N U L V E E**

    ⬡ ☐ ☐ ☐ ⬡

53. **R Y T R E A**

    ☐ ☐ ☐ ⬡ ☐ ☐

54. **U S L E P**

    ☐ ☐ ⬡ ☐ ☐

Take the circled letters, unscramble them, and fill in the solution.

How Noah survived the flood.

55. ☐ ☐ ☐ ☐ ☐ ☐ ☐

APPLYING WHAT YOU KNOW

56. Caryl is enjoying a picnic lunch when a bee suddenly flies down and stings her. Within seconds, Caryl begins to experience difficulty breathing, tachycardia, a decrease in blood pressure, and cyanosis. What is Caryl experiencing?

57. Wilson is scheduled to undergo extensive surgery. His surgeon, Dr. Berger, requests that 2 units of blood be available for Wilson should he require them. What complication of surgery is Dr. Berger hoping to avoid?

58. Rochelle is a hairstylist who works long hours. Lately she has noticed that her feet are sore and edematous. What might be the cause of these symptoms? What advice could offer Rochelle some relief from these symptoms?

59. Rubin returned from surgery in stable condition. The nurse noted that each time she took Rubin's pulse and blood pressure, the pulse was higher and the blood pressure lower than the last time. What might be the cause?

60. Word Find

Find and circle 15 terms presented in this chapter. Words may be spelled top to bottom, bottom to top, right to left, left to right, or diagonally.

Angina pectoris
Apex
Atrium
Depolarization
Diastolic
ECG
Endocardium
Hepatic portal

Pulse
Semilunar
Systemic
Thrombosis
Tricuspid
Umbilical
Venule

```
Y H Y S I S O B M O R H T A R
L A C I L I B M U O A Y N I Y
E E S Y S T E M I C C G D E U
M V E N U L E D D C I X M D I
E Y M U I R T A R N L E C G Y
N O I T A Z I R A L O P E D N
U D L A T R O P C I T A P E H
S I U K M U E T O E S L U P U
R P N F Y C B E D R A L Z P J
D S A H T I T V N L I I B D W
Q U R O I V A Q E O D A K R K
K C R M P G A I G N D D Z Y J
Y I Y R I N E A F Z L Q S P X
S R M I C C Q O A W U N H O K
P T A V H H Z L H I J J X K Z
```

KNOW YOUR MEDICAL TERMS

True or False

Indicate in the blank space if the literal translation is true or false for the medical term.

61. _____ Placenta means "flat cake."

62. _____ Tunica intima means "innermost coat."

63. _____ Aneurysm means "rupture."

64. _____ Gangrene means "black stump."

65. _____ Hemorrhoid means "vessel tightening."

66. _____ Necrosis means "death condition."

67. _____ Phlebitis means "vein inflammation."

68. _____ Sphygmomanometer means "a thin pulse measure."

69. _____ Varices means "swollen arteries."

70. _____ Septic shock means "relating to a putrid jolt."

▷ *If you had difficulty with this section, review pages 392 and 393.*

DID YOU KNOW?

- Every pound of excess fat contains 200 miles of additional capillaries.
- If laid out in a straight line, the average adult's circulatory system would be nearly 60,000 miles long—enough to circle the earth 2.5 times!

CIRCULATION OF THE BLOOD

Fill in the crossword puzzle.

ACROSS

2. Inflammation of the lining of the heart
3. Bicuspid valve (two words)
5. Inner layer of pericardium
7. Cardiopulmonary resuscitation (abbreviation)
10. Carries blood away from the heart
11. Upper chamber of heart
12. Lower chambers of the heart
13. SA node

DOWN

1. Unique blood circulation through the liver (two words)
3. Muscular layer of the heart
4. Carries blood to the heart
6. Tiny artery
8. Heart rate
9. Carries blood from arterioles into venules

CHECK YOUR KNOWLEDGE

Multiple Choice

Circle the correct answer.

1. The medical term for high blood pressure is:
   A. Arteriosclerosis
   B. Cyanosis
   C. Hypertension
   D. Central venous pressure

2. Septic shock is caused by:
   A. Complications of toxins in the blood
   B. A nerve condition
   C. A drop in blood pressure
   D. Blood vessel dilation

3. Hypovolemic shock is caused by:
   A. Heart failure
   B. Dilated blood vessels
   C. A drop in blood volume
   D. A severe allergic reaction

4. Which vessels collect blood from the capillaries and return it to the heart?
   A. Arteries
   B. Sinuses
   C. Veins
   D. Arterioles

5. The innermost coat of an artery that comes into direct contact with blood is called the:
   A. Lumen
   B. Tunica externa
   C. Tunica intima
   D. Tunica media

6. Hemorrhoids can best be described as:
   A. Varicose veins
   B. Varicose veins in the rectum
   C. Thrombophlebitis of the rectum
   D. Clot formation in the rectum

7. In the fetal circulation:
   A. The ductus venosus allows most blood from the placenta to bypass the fetal liver.
   B. The umbilical vein carries oxygen-poor blood.
   C. The foramen ovale connects the aorta and the pulmonary artery.
   D. None of the above is true.

8. Which of the following events, if any, would *not* cause the blood pressure to increase?
   A. Hemorrhaging
   B. Increasing the viscosity of the blood
   C. Increasing the strength of the heartbeat
   D. All of the above

9. Arteriosclerosis is a disorder of the:
   A. Heart
   B. Veins
   C. Capillaries
   D. Arteries

10. A common type of vascular disease that occludes arteries by lipids and other matter is:
    A. Arteriosclerotic plaque
    B. Atherosclerosis
    C. Varicose veins
    D. Thrombophlebitis

Matching

Match each description in column A with its corresponding term in column B. (There is only one correct answer for each item.)

Column A

_____ 11. Main artery

_____ 12. Decreased blood supply

_____ 13. Leg vein

_____ 14. Fetal circulation

_____ 15. Arterial procedure

_____ 16. Vein inflammation

_____ 17. Lung circulation

_____ 18. Weakened artery

_____ 19. Largest vein

_____ 20. Myocardial infarction

Column B

A. Ischemia

B. Phlebitis

C. Foramen ovale

D. Aneurysm

E. Vena cava

F. Angioplasty

G. Aorta

H. Pulmonary

I. Great saphenous vein

J. Cardiogenic shock

FETAL CIRCULATION

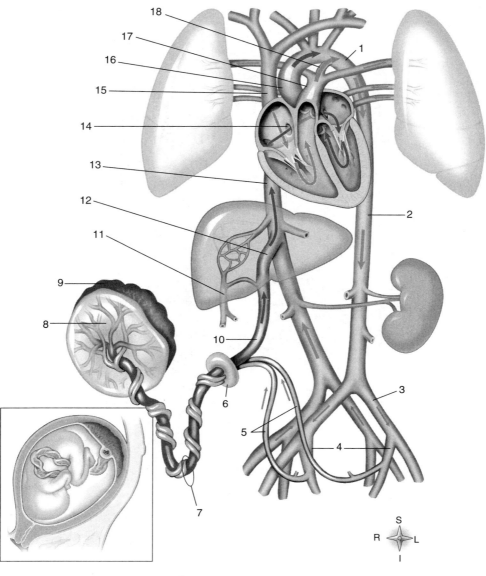

1. _____
2. _____
3. _____
4. _____
5. _____
6. _____
7. _____
8. _____
9. _____
10. _____
11. _____
12. _____
13. _____
14. _____
15. _____
16. _____
17. _____
18. _____

HEPATIC PORTAL CIRCULATION

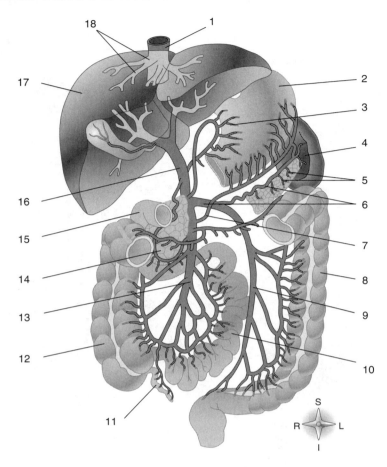

1. _____   10. _____

2. _____   11. _____

3. _____   12. _____

4. _____   13. _____

5. _____   14. _____

6. _____   15. _____

7. _____   16. _____

8. _____   17. _____

9. _____   18. _____

PRINCIPAL ARTERIES OF THE BODY

1. _____

2. _____

3. _____

4. _____

5. _____

6. _____

7. _____

8. _____

9. _____

10. _____

11. _____

12. _____

13. _____

14. _____

15. _____

16. _____

17. _____

18. _____

19. _____

20. _____

21. _____

22. _____

23. _____

24. _____

25. _____

26. _____

27. _____

28. _____

29. _____

30. _____

PRINCIPAL VEINS OF THE BODY

1. _____
2. _____
3. _____
4. _____
5. _____
6. _____
7. _____
8. _____
9. _____
10. _____
11. _____
12. _____
13. _____
14. _____
15. _____
16. _____
17. _____
18. _____
19. _____
20. _____
21. _____
22. _____
23. _____
24. _____
25. _____
26. _____
27. _____
28. _____
29. _____
30. _____
31. _____
32. _____
33. _____
34. _____
35. _____
36. _____
37. _____
38. _____

CHAPTER 16

The Lymphatic System and Immunity

The lymphatic system is similar to the circulatory system. Lymph, like blood, flows through an elaborate route of vessels. In addition to lymphatic vessels, the lymphatic system consists of lymph nodes, lymph, the thymus, tonsils, and the spleen. Unlike the circulatory system, the lymphatic vessels do not form a closed circuit. Lymph flows only once through the vessels before draining into the general blood circulation. This system is a filtering mechanism for microorganisms and serves as a protective device against foreign invaders such as cancer.

The immune system is the armed forces division of the body. Ready to attack at a moment's notice, the immune system defends us against the major enemies of the body: microorganisms, foreign transplanted tissue cells, and our own cells that have turned malignant.

The most numerous cells of the immune system are the lymphocytes. These cells circulate in the body's fluids seeking invading organisms and destroying them with powerful lymphotoxins, lymphokines, or antibodies.

Phagocytes, another large group of immune system cells, assist with the destruction of foreign invaders by a process known as *phagocytosis*. Neutrophils, monocytes, and connective tissue cells called *macrophages* use this process to surround unwanted microorganisms and ingest and digest them, rendering them harmless to the body.

Another weapon that the immune system possesses is complement. Normally a group of inactive enzymes present in the blood, complement can be activated to kill invading cells by drilling holes in their cytoplasmic membranes, which allows fluid to enter the cell until it bursts.

Your review of this chapter will give you an understanding of how the body defends itself from the daily invasion of destructive substances.

TOPICS FOR REVIEW

Before progressing to Chapter 17, you should familiarize yourself with the functions of the lymphatic system, the immune system, and the major structures that make up these systems. Your review should include knowledge of lymphatic vessels, lymph nodes, lymph, lymphatic organs and tissues, antibodies, complement, and the development of B and T cells. Your study should also include the differences in humoral and cell-mediated immunity. Finally, an understanding of the excessive responses of the immune system and immune system deficiencies are necessary to complete your review of this chapter.

THE LYMPHATIC SYSTEM

Fill in the blanks.

1. _____ is a specialized fluid formed in the tissue spaces that will be transported by way of specialized vessels to eventually reenter the circulatory system.

2. Blood plasma that has filtered out of capillaries into microscopic spaces between cells is called _____ _____.

3. Tiny blind-ended tubes distributed in the tissue spaces are called _____ _____.

4. Lymph eventually empties into two terminal vessels called the _____ _____ _____ and the _____ _____.

5. The thoracic duct has an enlarged pouchlike structure called the _____ _____.

6. Lymph is filtered by moving through _____ _____, which are located in clusters along the pathway of lymphatic vessels.

7. Lymph enters the node through four _____ lymph vessels.

8. Lymph exits the node through a single _____ lymph vessel.

9. An abnormal condition in which tissues exhibit edema because of the accumulation of lymph is _____.

10. Hodgkin disease is an example of _____.

▶ *If you had difficulty with this section, review pages 415-422.*

THYMUS

TONSILS

SPLEEN

Match each numbered description to one of the lymphatic system structures. Write the corresponding letter in the answer blank.

A. Thymus   B. Tonsils   C. Spleen

_____ 11. Palatine, pharyngeal, and lingual are examples

_____ 12. The largest lymphoid organ in the body

_____ 13. Destroys worn-out red blood cells

_____ 14. Located in the mediastinum

_____ 15. Serves as a reservoir for blood

_____ 16. T lymphocytes

_____ 17. Largest at puberty

▶ *If you had difficulty with this section, review pages 422-423.*

THE IMMUNE SYSTEM

Match each term on the left with its corresponding description on the right.

_____ 18. Nonspecific immunity

_____ 19. Phagocytes

_____ 20. Specific immunity

_____ 21. Lymphocytes

_____ 22. Immunization

A. Innate immunity

B. Acquired immunity

C. General protection

D. Artificial active immunity

E. Memory

IMMUNE SYSTEM MOLECULES

Match each description with its related term. Write the corresponding letter in the answer blank.

_____ 23. A type of very specific antibody produced from a population of identical cells

_____ 24. Protein compounds normally present in the body

_____ 25. Also known as *antibody-mediated immunity*

_____ 26. Combines with antibody to produce humoral immunity

_____ 27. Antibody

_____ 28. The process of changing antibody molecule shape slightly to expose binding sites

_____ 29. Capable of producing large quantities of very specific antibodies

_____ 30. Inactive proteins in blood

A. Antibodies

B. Antigen

C. Monoclonal

D. Complement cascade

E. Complement

F. Humoral

G. Combining site

H. Hybridomas

▷ *If you had difficulty with this section, review pages 423-428.*

IMMUNE SYSTEM CELLS

Circle the correct answer.

31. The most numerous cells of the immune system are the:
    A. Monocytes
    B. Eosinophils
    C. Neutrophils
    D. Lymphocytes
    E. Complement

32. The second stage of B-cell development changes a mature inactive B cell into a/an:
    A. Plasma cell
    B. Stem cell
    C. Antibody
    D. Activated B cell
    E. Immature B cell

33. Which one of the following is activated last in the immune process?
    A. Plasma cells
    B. Stem cells
    C. Antibodies
    D. Activated B cells
    E. Immature B cells

34. Which one of the following is part of the cell membrane of B cells?
    A. Complement
    B. Antigens
    C. Antibodies
    D. Epitopes
    E. None of the above

35. Immature B cells have:
    A. Four types of defense mechanisms on their cell membrane
    B. Several kinds of defense mechanisms on their cell membrane
    C. One specific kind of defense mechanism on their cell membrane
    D. No defense mechanisms on their cell membrane

36. Development of an active B cell depends on the B cell coming in contact with:
    A. Complement
    B. Antibodies
    C. Lymphotoxins
    D. Lymphokines
    E. Antigens

37. The kind of cell that produces large numbers of antibodies is the:
    A. B cell
    B. Stem cell
    C. T cell
    D. Memory cell
    E. Plasma cell

38. Just one of these short-lived cells that make antibodies can produce _____ of them per second.
    A. 20
    B. 200
    C. 2000
    D. 20,000

39. Which of the following statements is *not* true of memory cells?
    A. They can secrete antibodies.
    B. They are found in lymph nodes.
    C. They develop into plasma cells.
    D. They can react with antigens.
    E. All of the above are true of memory cells.

40. T-cell development begins in the:
    A. Lymph nodes
    B. Liver
    C. Pancreas
    D. Spleen
    E. Thymus

41. B cells function indirectly to produce:
    A. Humoral immunity
    B. Cell-mediated immunity
    C. Lymphotoxins
    D. Lymphokines

42. T cells function to produce:
    A. Humoral immunity
    B. Cell-mediated immunity
    C. Antibodies
    D. Memory cells

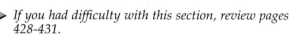 *If you had difficulty with this section, review pages 428-431.*

HYPERSENSITIVITY OF THE IMMUNE SYSTEM

Circle the correct answer.

43. The term *allergy* is used to describe (*hypersensitivity* or *hyposensitivity*) of the immune system to relatively harmless environmental antigens.

44. Antigens that trigger an allergic response are often called (*antibodies* or *allergens*).

45. (*Anaphylactic shock* or *Urticaria*) is a life-threatening condition.

46. A common autoimmune disease is (*lupus* or *SCID*).

47. Erythroblastosis fetalis is an example of (*isoimmunity* or *autoimmunity*).

48. The antigens most commonly involved in transplant rejection are called (*SCIDs* or *HLAs*).

If you had difficulty with this section, review pages 431-434.

IMMUNE DEFICIENCY

Match each condition with its origin. Write the corresponding letter in the answer blank.

A. Congenital   B.   Acquired (after birth)

_____ 49. AIDS

_____ 50. SCID

_____ 51. Improper B-cell development

_____ 52. Viral infection

_____ 53. Genetic defect

▶ *If you had difficulty with this section, review pages 434-436.*

UNSCRAMBLE THE WORDS

54. **N T C M P E O L E M**

55. **M T M Y I U N I**

56. **O E N C L S**

57. **F N R O E R T E N I**

Take the circled letters, unscramble them, and fill in the solution.

What the student was praying for the night before exams.

58.

...and please, don't let me forget to remember!

APPLYING WHAT YOU KNOW

59. Two-year-old baby Metcalfe was exposed to chickenpox and subsequently developed the disease. What type of immunity will be developed as a result of this?

60. Marcia was an intravenous drug user. She has developed a type of skin cancer known as Kaposi sarcoma. What is Marcia's probable primary diagnosis?

61. Baby Wilson is born without a thymus gland. Immediate plans are made for a transplant to be performed. In the meantime, baby Wilson is placed in strict isolation. For what reason is he placed in isolation?

62. Word Find

Find and circle 14 terms presented in this chapter. Words may be spelled top to bottom, bottom to top, right to left, left to right, or diagonally.

Acquired	Lymphocytes
Antigen	Macrophage
Humoral	Monoclonal
Immunity	Proteins
Inflammatory	Spleen
Interferon	Thymus
Lymph	Tonsils

```
I  N  F  L  A  M  M  A  T  O  R  Y  F  C  G
Q  N  L  O  Y  Z  O  C  C  P  A  O  F  S  X
M  W  T  A  A  M  N  J  X  Q  K  R  N  P  H
U  R  L  E  R  M  P  X  B  R  U  I  A  L  C
C  M  A  C  R  O  P  H  A  G  E  I  E  D  Z
X  M  N  D  K  F  M  N  O  T  U  C  R  N  M
A  E  O  R  E  Z  E  U  O  C  F  B  Y  E  B
Y  P  L  E  B  G  G  R  H  T  Y  T  S  E  D
Y  S  C  R  I  S  P  J  O  E  I  T  M  L  A
Z  M  O  T  J  X  E  T  O  N  A  E  E  P  X
T  O  N  S  I  L  S  S  U  M  Y  H  T  S  Y
W  A  O  C  J  N  I  M  W  K  O  Z  E  N  D
D  W  M  K  W  R  M  O  I  P  S  H  Y  B  G
F  H  W  U  J  I  Z  F  V  D  Z  L  Y  T  X
```

KNOW YOUR MEDICAL TERMS

Provide the literal translation for the following words.

63. Cisterna chyli _____

64. Clone _____

65. Efferent _____

66. Lacteal _____

67. Thymus _____

68. Adenoid _____

69. Hypersensitivity _____

70. Lymphedema _____

71. Vaccine _____

72. Tonsillitis _____

▷ *If you had difficulty with this section, review pages 416 and 417.*

DID YOU KNOW?

- In the United States, the HIV infection rate is increasing four times faster in women than in men. Women tend to underestimate their risk.
- Ten percent of all HIV/AIDS cases are individuals 50 years of age and older.

LYMPH AND IMMUNITY

Fill in the crossword puzzle.

ACROSS

1. Largest lymphoid organ in the body
3. Connective tissue cells that are phagocytes
4. Protein compounds normally present in the body
5. Remain in reserve, then turn into plasma cells when needed (two words)
9. Synthetically produced to fight certain diseases
10. Lymph exits the node through this lymph vessel

11. Lymph enters the node through these lymph vessels

DOWN

2. Secretes a copious amount of antibodies into the blood (two words)
6. Inactive proteins
7. Family of identical cells descended from one cell
8. Type of lymphocyte (humoral immunity—two words)
11. Immune deficiency disorder

12. Type of lymphocyte (cell-mediated immunity—two words)

CHECK YOUR KNOWLEDGE

Multiple Choice

Circle the correct answer.

1. T cells do which of the following?
   A. Develop in the thymus
   B. Form memory cells
   C. Form plasma cells
   D. All of the above

2. Lymph does which of the following?
   A. Forms as blood plasma filters out of capillaries
   B. Empties into the heart
   C. Flows through lymphatic arteries
   D. All of the above

3. Acquired immune deficiency syndrome is characterized by which of the following?
   A. Caused by a retrovirus
   B. Causes inadequate T-cell formation
   C. Can result in death from cancer or infection
   D. All of the above

4. Interferon is:
   A. Produced by B cells
   B. A protein compound that protects other cells by interfering with the ability of a virus to reproduce
   C. A group of inactive enzyme proteins normally present in blood
   D. All of the above

5. B cells do which of the following?
   A. Develop into plasma cells and memory cells
   B. Establish humoral immunity
   √C. Develop from primitive cells in bone marrow called *stem cells*
   D. All of the above

6. Which of the following functions to kill invading cells by drilling a hole in the plasma membrane?
   A. Interferon
   B. Complement cascade
   C. Antibody
   D. Memory cell

7. Which of the following cell types function in the immune system?
   A. Macrophages
   B. Lymphocytes
   C. T cells
   D. All of the above

8. Which of the following is an example of phagocytes?
   A. Dendritic cells
   B. Neutrophils
   C. Macrophages
   D. All of the above

9. What is a rapidly growing population of identical cells that produce large quantities of specific antibodies called?
   A. Complementary
   B. Lymphotoxic
   C. Chemotactic
   D. Monoclonal

10. Which of the following is a form of passive natural immunity?
    A. A child develops measles and acquires an immunity to subsequent infection.
    B. Antibodies are injected into an infected individual.
    C. An infant receives protection through its mother's milk.
    D. Vaccinations are given against smallpox.

Matching

Match each of the terms in column A with its corresponding description in column B. (Only one answer is correct for each.)

Column A

_____ 11. Adenoids

_____ 12. B cell

_____ 13. Clone

_____ 14. HIV virus

_____ 15. Complement

_____ 16. Filtration

_____ 17. Cisterna chyli

_____ 18. T cell

_____ 19. Vaccination

_____ 20. Antigen

Column B

A. Thoracic duct

B. Lymph node

C. Artificial immunity

D. Humoral immunity

E. Pharyngeal tonsils

F. Shaped to combine with an antibody

G. Inactive proteins

H. AIDS

I. Identical cells

J. Cell-mediated immunity

PRINCIPAL ORGANS OF THE LYMPHATIC SYSTEM

1. _____

2. _____

3. _____

4. _____

5. _____

6. _____

7. _____

8. _____

9. _____

10. _____

11. _____

12. _____

13. _____

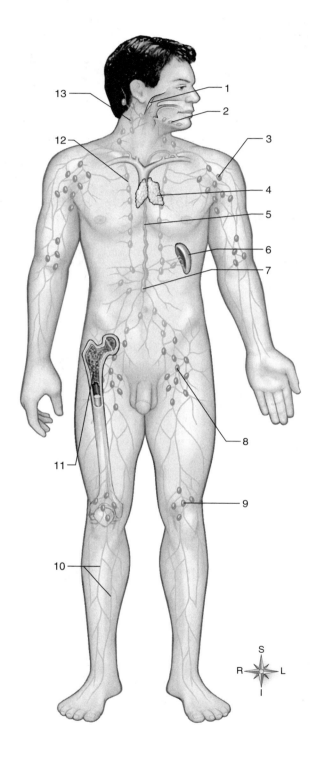

CHAPTER 17

The Respiratory System

As you sit reviewing this system, your body needs 16 quarts of air per minute. Walking requires 24 quarts of air, and running requires 50 quarts per minute. The respiratory system provides the air necessary for you to perform your daily activities and eliminates the waste gases from the air that you breathe. Take a deep breath, and think of the air as entering some 250 million tiny air sacs similar in appearance to clusters of grapes. These microscopic air sacs expand to let air in and contract to force it out. These tiny sacs, or alveoli, are the functioning units of the respiratory system. They provide the necessary volume of oxygen and eliminate carbon dioxide 24 hours a day.

Air enters either through the mouth or the nasal cavity. It next passes through the pharynx and past the epiglottis, through the glottis and the rest of the larynx. It then continues down the trachea, into the bronchi to the bronchioles, and finally through the alveoli. The reverse occurs for expelled air.

The exchange of gases between air in the lungs and in the blood is known as *external respiration*. The exchange of gases that occurs between the blood and the cells of the body is known as *internal respiration*. By constantly supplying adequate oxygen and removing carbon dioxide as it forms, the respiratory system helps maintain an environment conducive to maximum cell efficiency.

Your review of this system is necessary to provide you with an understanding of this essential homeostatic mechanism that supplies oxygen to our cells.

TOPICS FOR REVIEW

Before progressing to Chapter 18, you should have an understanding of the structure and function of the organs of the respiratory system. Your review should include knowledge of the mechanisms responsible for both internal and external respiration. Your study should conclude with a knowledge of the volumes of air exchanged in pulmonary ventilation, an understanding of how respiration is regulated, and the common disorders of the respiratory tract.

STRUCTURAL PLAN

RESPIRATORY TRACT

RESPIRATORY MUCOSA

Match each term with its definition. Write the corresponding letter in the answer blank.

_____ 1. Function of respiratory system	A. Diffusion
_____ 2. Pharynx	B. Respiratory membrane
_____ 3. Passive transport process responsible for actual exchange of gases	C. Alveoli
	D. Capillaries
_____ 4. Assists with the movement of mucus toward the pharynx	E. Respiration
_____ 5. Barrier between the blood in the capillaries and the air in the alveolus	F. Respiratory mucosa
	G. Upper respiratory tract
_____ 6. Lines the tubes of the respiratory tree	H. Lower respiratory tract
_____ 7. Terminal air sacs	I. Cilia
_____ 8. Trachea	J. Air distributor
_____ 9. Surround alveoli	
_____ 10. Homeostatic mechanism	

Fill in the blanks.

The organs of the respiratory system are designed to perform two basic functions. They serve as an

(11) _____ _____ and as a

(12) _____ _____. In addition to the

functions given above, the respiratory system (13) _____,

(14) _____, and (15) _____ the air we

breathe. Respiratory organs include the (16) _____,

(17) _____, (18) _____,

(19) _____, (20) _____, and the

(21) _____. The respiratory system ends in millions of tiny, thin-walled

sacs called (22) _____. (23) _____ of

gases takes place in these sacs. Two aspects of the structure of these sacs assist them in the exchange of

gases. First, an extremely thin membrane, the (24) _____

_____, allows for easy exchange, and second, the large number of air

sacs makes an enormous (25) _____ area.

▶ *If you had difficulty with this section, review pages 442-448.*

NOSE

PHARYNX

LARYNX

DISORDERS OF UPPER RESPIRATORY TRACT

Circle the term in each word group that does not belong.

26. Nares   Septum   Oropharynx   Conchae

27. Conchae   Frontal   Maxillary   Sphenoidal

28. Oropharynx   Throat   5 inches   Epiglottis

29. Pharyngeal   Adenoids   Uvula   Nasopharynx

30. Middle ear   Tubes   Nasopharynx   Larynx

31. Voice box   Thyroid cartilage   Tonsils   Vocal cords

32. Palatine   Eustachian tube   Tonsils   Oropharynx

33. Pharynx   Epiglottis   Adam's apple   Voice box

Match each numbered term or phrase with the corresponding respiratory structure.

A. Nose   B. Pharynx   C. Larynx

_____ 34. Warms and humidifies air

_____ 35. Air and food pass through here

_____ 36. Sinuses

_____ 37. Conchae

_____ 38. Septum

_____ 39. Tonsils

_____ 40. Middle ear infections

_____ 41. Epiglottis

_____ 42. Rhinitis

_____ 43. Sore throat

_____ 44. Epistaxis (nose bleed)

▶ *If you had difficulty with this section, review pages 448-453.*

TRACHEA

BRONCHI, BRONCHIOLES, AND ALVEOLI

LUNGS AND PLEURA

Fill in the blanks.

45. The windpipe is more properly referred to as the _____.

46. _____ ensure that the framework of the trachea is almost noncollapsible.

47. A life-saving technique designed to free the trachea of ingested food or foreign objects is the

_____ _____.

48. The first branch or division of the trachea leading to the lungs is the _____

   _____.

49. Each alveolar duct ends in several _____ _____.

50. The narrow part of each lung, up under the collarbone, is its _____.

51. The _____ covers the outer surface of the lungs and lines the inner surface of the rib cage.

52. Inflammation of the lining of the thoracic cavity is _____.

53. The presence of air in the pleural space on one side of the chest is a _____.

▷ *If you had difficulty with this section, review pages 453-457.*

RESPIRATION

True or False

If the statement is true, write "T" in the answer blank. If the statement is false, correct the statement by circling the incorrect term and writing the correct term in the answer blank.

___F Pulmonary ventilation___ 54. Diffusion is the process that moves air into and out of the lungs.

___F Expiration___ 55. For inspiration to take place, the diaphragm and other respiratory muscles must relax.

___F down___ 56. Diffusion is a passive process that results in movement up a concentration gradient.

___F internal___ 57. The exchange of gases that occurs between blood in tissue capillaries and the body cells is external respiration.

___T___ 58. Many different pulmonary volumes can be measured by having a person breathe into a spirometer.

___F 1 pint___ 59. Ordinarily we take about 2 pints of air into our lungs with each breath.

___T___ 60. The amount of air normally breathed in and out with each breath is called tidal volume.

___F vital capacity___ 61. The largest amount of air that one can breathe out in one expiration is called residual volume.

___T___ 62. The inspiratory reserve volume is the amount of air that can be forcibly inhaled after a normal inspiration.

▷ *If you had difficulty with this section, review pages 457-462.*

Circle the correct answer.

63. The term that means the same thing as breathing is:
   A. Gas exchange
   B. Respiration
   C. Inspiration
   D. Expiration
   E. Pulmonary ventilation

64. Carbaminohemoglobin is formed when _____ bind(s) to hemoglobin.
   A. Oxygen
   B. Amino acids
   C. Carbon dioxide
   D. Nitrogen
   E. None of the above

65. Most of the oxygen transported by the blood is:
    A. Dissolved into white blood cells
    B. Bound to white blood cells
    C. Bound to hemoglobin
    D. Bound to carbaminohemoglobin
    E. None of the above

66. Which of the following does *not* occur during inspiration?
    A. Elevation of the ribs
    B. Elevation of the diaphragm
    C. Contraction of the diaphragm
    D. Elongation of the chest cavity from top to bottom

67. A young adult male would have a vital capacity of about _____ ml.
    A. 500
    B. 1200
    C. 3300
    D. 4800
    E. 6200

68. The amount of air that can be forcibly exhaled after expiring the tidal volume is known as the:
    A. Total lung capacity
    B. Vital capacity
    C. Inspiratory reserve volume
    D. Expiratory reserve volume
    E. None of the above

69. Which one of the following formulas is correct?
    A. $VC = TV - IRV + ERV$
    B. $VC = TV + IRV - ERV$
    C. $VC = TV + IRV \times ERV$
    D. $VC = TV + IRV + ERV$
    E. None of the above

▶ *If you had difficulty with this section, review pages 457-462.*

REGULATION OF RESPIRATION

BREATHING PATTERNS

Match each term on the left with the corresponding description on the right.

_____ 70. Respiratory control centers
_____ 71. Chemoreceptors
_____ 72. Pulmonary stretch receptors
_____ 73. Dyspnea
_____ 74. Respiratory arrest
_____ 75. Eupnea
_____ 76. Hypoventilation

A. Difficult breathing
B. Located in carotid bodies
C. Slow and shallow respirations
D. Normal respiratory rate
E. Located in the brainstem
F. Failure to resume breathing after a period of apnea
G. Located throughout pulmonary airways and in the alveoli

▶ *If you had difficulty with this section, review pages 462-464.*

DISORDERS OF THE LOWER RESPIRATORY TRACT

Fill in the blanks.

77. _____ is an acute inflammation of the lungs in which the alveoli and bronchi become plugged with thick fluid.

78. _____ is still a major cause of death in many poor, densely populated regions of the world. It has recently reemerged as an important health problem in some major U.S. cities.

79. _____ may result from the progression of chronic bronchitis or other conditions as air becomes trapped within alveoli, causing them to enlarge and eventually rupture.

80. _____ is an obstructive disorder characterized by recurring spasms of the smooth muscle in the walls of the bronchial air passages.

▶ *If you had difficulty with this section, review pages 464-468.*

UNSCRAMBLE THE WORDS

81. **S P U E L I R Y**

⬭☐☐⬭⬭☐☐

82. **C R N B O S I T H I**

☐☐☐⬭⬭☐☐⬭☐☐☐

83. **S E S X P T I A I**

☐☐☐⬭⬭☐☐⬭☐☐

84. **D D N E A O I S**

⬭☐☐⬭☐☐☐

Take the circled letters, unscramble them, and fill in the solution.

What Mona Lisa was to DaVinci.

85. ☐☐☐☐☐☐☐☐☐☐☐☐☐

APPLYING WHAT YOU KNOW

86. Mr. Gorski is a heavy smoker. Recently he has noticed that when he gets up in the morning, he has a bothersome cough that brings up a large accumulation of mucus. This cough persists for several minutes and then leaves until the next morning. What is an explanation for this problem?

87. Penny is 5 years old and is a mouth breather. She has had repeated episodes of tonsillitis, and her pediatrician, Dr. Smith, has suggested removal of her tonsils and adenoids. He further suggests that the surgery will probably cure her mouth breathing problem. Why is this a possibility?

88. Sandy developed emphysema. This disease reduces the capacity of the lungs to recoil elastically. Which respiratory air volumes will this condition affect? Why?

DID YOU KNOW?

- If the alveoli in our lungs were flattened out, they would cover one-half of a tennis court.
- Eighty percent of lung cancer cases are due to cigarette smoking.
- Only about 10% of the air in the lungs is actually changed with each cycle of inhaling and exhaling when a person at-rest is breathing. However, up to 80% can be exchanged during deep breathing or strenuous exercise.
- A person's nose and ears continue to grow throughout his or her life.

89. Word Find

Find and circle 14 terms presented in this chapter. Words may be spelled top to bottom, bottom to top, right to left, left to right, or diagonally.

Adenoids
Carotid body
Cilia
Diffusion
Dyspnea
Epiglottis
Hypoventilation

Inspiration
Oxyhemoglobin
Pulmonary
Residual volume
Surfactant
URI
Vital capacity

```
N K S A Q B I L V A D T I X D
O X O O B F I F G I M N R G Y
I G N X W D E E F L B A U T S
T B K Y N H E F O I U T I R P
A T M H E O U T R C C C P V N
L L A E P S I R I Z A A N F E
I P T M I H G T I P R F P C A
T U B O G Q E V A Q O R V N W
N L N G L R J C C R T U P D C
E M U L O V L A U D I S E R E
V O V O T A N G J E D P Z U U
O N K B T C N U U E B O S J S
P A L I I K E U C N O Z K N A
Y R V N S D I O N E D A M F I
H Y O M L O A Z D T Y M N L K
```

KNOW YOUR MEDICAL TERMS

Matching

Select the medical term with matching literal translation.

90. _____ Alveolus
91. _____ Diffusion
92. _____ Olfaction
93. _____ Apnea
94. _____ Epiglottis
95. _____ Asthma
96. _____ Sinus
97. _____ Pleura
98. _____ Epistaxis
99. _____ Rhinitis
100. _____ Emphysema

A. Upon/mouth of windpipe
B. Hollow
C. Spread out/process
D. Side of body
E. Panting
F. Hollow/little
G. Not/breathe/condition
H. Upon/drip
I. Smell/condition
J. Nose/inflammation
K. In/blowing or puffing up

▷ *If you had difficulty with this section, review pages 444-446.*

RESPIRATORY SYSTEM

Fill in the crossword puzzle.

ACROSS

1. Device used to measure the amount of air exchanged in breathing
6. Expiratory reserve volume (abbreviation)
7. Sphenoidal _____ (two words)
8. Terminal air sacs
9. Shelflike structures that protrude into the nasal cavity
11. Inflammation of pleura
12. Respirations stop

DOWN

2. Surgical procedure to remove tonsils
3. Doctor who developed life-saving technique
4. Windpipe
5. Trachea branches into right and left structures
10. Voice box

CHECK YOUR KNOWLEDGE

Multiple Choice

Circle the correct answer.

1. Chemoreceptors in the carotid and aortic bodies are characterized by which of the following?
   A. Sensitive to increases in blood carbon dioxide level
   B. Found in the brain
   C. Sensitive to increases in blood oxygen level
   D. Send impulses to the heart

2. What is the lowest segment of the pharynx called?
   A. Oropharynx
   B. Laryngopharynx
   C. Nasopharynx
   D. Hypopharynx

3. What is the narrow upper portion of a lung called?
   A. Base
   B. Notch
   C. Costal surface
   D. Apex

4. What is the largest amount of air that a person can breathe in and out in one inspiration and expiration called?
   A. Tidal volume
   B. Vital capacity
   C. Residual volume
   D. Inspiratory reserve volume

5. Which of the following statements, if any, is *not* characteristic of human lungs?
   A. Both right and left lungs are composed of three lobes.
   B. Bronchi subdivide to form bronchioles.
   C. Capillary supply is abundant to facilitate gas exchange.
   D. All of the above statements are characteristic of human lungs.

6. Which body function is made possible by the existence of fibrous bands stretched across the larynx?
   A. Swallowing
   B. Breathing
   C. Diffusion
   D. Speech

7. The trachea is almost noncollapsible because of the presence of which of the following?
   A. Rings of cartilage
   B. Thyroid cartilage
   C. Epiglottis
   D. Vocal cords

8. Which of the following is true of the exchange of respiratory gases between lungs and blood?
   A. It takes place by diffusion.
   B. It is called *external respiration*.
   C. Both A and B are true.
   D. None of the above is true.

9. When the diaphragm contracts, which phase of ventilation is taking place?
   A. External respiration
   B. Expiration
   C. Internal respiration
   D. Inspiration

10. Which of the following is *not* characteristic of the nasal cavities?
    A. They contain many blood vessels that warm incoming air.
    B. They contain the adenoids.
    C. They are lined with mucous membranes.
    D. They are separated by a partition called the *nasal septum*.

Matching

Match each term in column A with its corresponding term in column B. (Only one answer is correct for each.)

Column A

_____ 11. Vocal cords

_____ 12. Pulmonary ventilation

_____ 13. Pleura

_____ 14. Atelectasis

_____ 15. Emphysema

_____ 16. Throat

_____ 17. Ethmoidal

_____ 18. Windpipe

_____ 19. Alveoli

_____ 20. Surfactant

Column B

A. Serous membrane

B. Pharynx

C. Paranasal sinus

D. LVRS

E. Larynx

F. Diffusion

G. Collapsed lung

H. Trachea

I. Breathing

J. IRDS

SAGITTAL VIEW OF FACE AND NECK

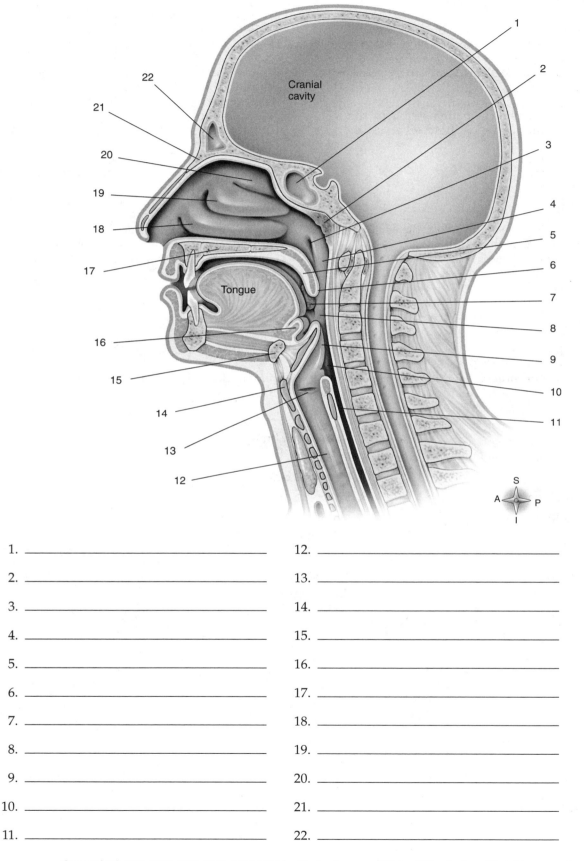

1. _____

2. _____

3. _____

4. _____

5. _____

6. _____

7. _____

8. _____

9. _____

10. _____

11. _____

12. _____

13. _____

14. _____

15. _____

16. _____

17. _____

18. _____

19. _____

20. _____

21. _____

22. _____

RESPIRATORY ORGANS

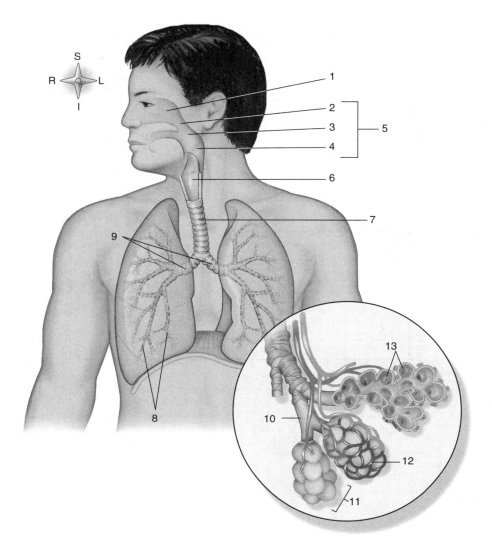

1. _____

2. _____

3. _____

4. _____

5. _____

6. _____

7. _____

8. _____

9. _____

10. _____

11. _____

12. _____

13. _____

PULMONARY VENTILATION VOLUMES

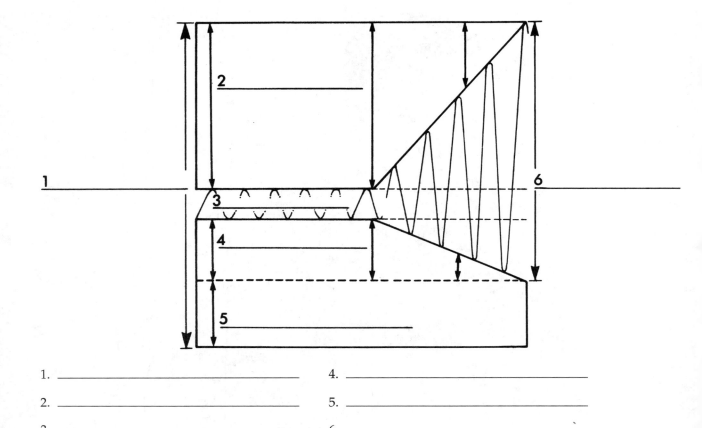

1. _____   4. _____

2. _____   5. _____

3. _____   6. _____

CHAPTER 18

The Digestive System

Think of the last meal you ate. Imagine the different shapes, sizes, tastes, and textures that you so recently enjoyed. Think of those items circulating in your bloodstream in those same original shapes, sizes, and textures. Impossible? Of course! Because of this impossibility, you can begin to understand and marvel at the close relationship of the digestive system to the circulatory system. It is the digestive system that changes our food, both mechanically and chemically, into a form that can be used by the blood and the body.

This change in food begins the moment you take the very first bite. Digestion starts in the mouth, where food is chewed and mixed with saliva. It then moves down the pharynx and esophagus by peristalsis and enters the stomach. In the stomach it is churned and mixed with gastric juices to become chyme. The chyme goes from the stomach into the duodenum where it is further broken down chemically by intestinal fluids, bile, and pancreatic juice. Those secretions prepare the food for absorption all along the course of the small intestine. Products that are not absorbed pass on through the entire length of the small intestine (duodenum, jejunum, ileum). From there they enter into the cecum of the large intestine, continue on to the ascending colon, transverse colon, descending colon, and sigmoid colon, and finally into the rectum, and out the anus.

Products that are used in the cells undergo absorption. Absorption allows newly processed nutrients to pass through the walls of the digestive tract and into the bloodstream to be distributed to the cells.

Your review of this system will help you understand the mechanical and chemical processes necessary to convert food into energy sources and compounds necessary for survival.

TOPICS FOR REVIEW

Before progressing to Chapter 19, you should review the structure and function of all the organs of digestion. You should have an understanding of the process of digestion, both chemical and mechanical, and of the processes of absorption and metabolism.

THE DIGESTIVE SYSTEM

ORGANS OF THE DIGESTIVE SYSTEM

Fill in the blanks.

1. The organs of the digestive system form an irregular-shaped tube called the *alimentary canal* or, as it is often called, the ___gastrointestinal___ ___tract___.

2. The churning of food in the stomach is an example of the ___digestion___ breakdown of food.

3. ___Chemical___ breakdown occurs when digestive enzymes act on food as it passes through the digestive tract.

4. Waste material resulting from the digestive process is known as ___Feces___.

5. Foods undergo three kinds of processing in the body: ___digestion___, ___absorption___, and ___metabolism___.

Identify which are main organs and which are accessory organs of the digestive system. Write the corresponding letter in the answer blank.

A. Main organ   B. Accessory organ

__A__ 6. Mouth   __A__ 13. Pharynx

__B__ 7. Parotids   __B__ 14. Appendix

__B__ 8. Liver   __A__ 15. Teeth

__A__ 9. Stomach   __B__ 16. Gallbladder

__A__ 10. Cecum   __B__ 17. Pancreas

__A__ 11. Esophagus

__A__ 12. Rectum   ▶ *If you had difficulty with this section, review pages 475-479.*

MOUTH

TEETH

SALIVARY GLANDS

Circle the correct answer.

18. Which one of the following is *not* a part of the roof of the mouth?
    A. Uvula ✓
    B. Palatine bones ✓
    C. Maxillary bones ✓
    D. Soft palate ✓
    E. All of the above are part of the roof of the mouth.

19. The largest of the papillae on the surface of the tongue are the:
    A. Filiform
    B. Fungiform
    C. Circumvallate
    D. Taste buds

20. The first baby tooth, on average, appears at:
    A. 2 months
    B. 1 year
    C. 3 months
    D. 1 month
    E. 6 months

21. The portion of the tooth that is covered with enamel is the:
    A. Pulp cavity
    B. Neck
    C. Root
    D. Crown
    E. None of the above is correct.

22. The wall of the pulp cavity is surrounded by:
    A. Enamel
    B. Dentin
    C. Cementum
    D. Connective tissue
    E. Blood and lymphatic vessels

23. Which of the following teeth is missing from the deciduous arch?
    A. Central incisor
    B. Canine
    C. Second premolar
    D. First molar
    E. Second molar

24. The permanent central incisor erupts between the ages of _____.
    A. 9 and 13
    B. 5 and 6
    C. 7 and 10
    D. 7 and 8
    E. None of the above

25. The third molar appears between the ages of _____.
    A. 10 and 14
    B. 5 and 8
    C. 11 and 16
    D. 17 and 24
    E. None of the above

26. A general term for infection of the gums is:
    A. Dental caries
    B. Leukoplakia
    C. Vincent angina
    D. Gingivitis

27. The ducts of the _____ glands open into the floor of the mouth.
    A. Sublingual
    B. Submandibular
    C. Parotid
    D. Carotid

28. The volume of saliva secreted per day is about:
    A. One-half pint
    B. One pint
    C. One liter
    D. One gallon

29. Mumps are an infection of the:
    A. Parotid gland
    B. Sublingual gland
    C. Submandibular gland
    D. Tonsils

30. Incisors are used during mastication to:
    A. Cut
    B. Pierce
    C. Tear
    D. Grind

31. Another name for the third molar is:
    A. Central incisor
    B. Wisdom tooth
    C. Canine
    D. Lateral incisor

32. After food has been chewed, it is formed into a small rounded mass called a:
    A. Moat
    B. Chyme
    C. Bolus
    D. Protease

▶ *If you had difficulty with this section, review pages 479-485.*

WALL OF DIGESTIVE TRACT

Fill in the blanks.

33. The serosa of the digestive tube is composed of the __Visceral peritoneum__ in the abdominal cavity.

34. The digestive tract extends from the __mouth__ to the __anus__.

35. The inside or hollow space within the alimentary canal is called the __lumen__.

36. The inside layer of the digestive tract is the ~~mucosa~~ small intestine

37. The connective tissue layer that lies beneath the lining of the digestive tract is the ~~serosa~~ submucosa

38. The muscularis contracts and moves food through the gastrointestinal tract by a process known as
    <u>peristalsis</u>.

39. The outermost covering of the digestive tube is the <u>serosa</u>.

40. The loops of the digestive tract are anchored to the posterior wall of the abdominal cavity by the
    <u>mesentery</u>.

PHARYNX

ESOPHAGUS

STOMACH

Fill in the blanks.

The (41) <u>pharynx</u> is a tubelike structure that functions as part of both the respiratory and digestive systems. It connects the mouth with the (42) <u>anus</u>.
The esophagus serves as a passageway for movement of food from the pharynx to the
(43) <u>stomach</u>. Food enters the stomach by passing through the muscular
(44) <u>lower</u> <u>esophageal</u>
<u>sphincter</u> at the end of the esophagus. Contraction of the stomach mixes the
food thoroughly with the gastric juices and breaks it down into a semisolid mixture called
(45) <u>chyme</u>. The three divisions of the stomach are the
(46) <u>fundus</u>, (47) <u>body</u>, and
(48) <u>pylorus</u>. Food is held in the stomach by the
(49) <u>pyloric sphincter</u> muscle long enough
for partial digestion to occur. After food has been in the stomach for approximately 3 hours, the chyme will enter
the (50) <u>small intestine</u>.

Match each term with its corresponding definition.

D	51. Stomach folds	A. Esophagus
J	52. Upper right border of stomach	B. Chyme
G	53. Heartburn	C. Peristalsis
A	54. 10-inch passageway	D. Rugae
H	55. Vomiting	E. Ulcer
B	56. Semisolid mixture of stomach contents	F. Greater curvature
C	57. Muscle contractions of the digestive system	G. Acid indigestion
E	58. Craterlike wound in digestive system caused by tissue destruction	H. Emesis
I	59. Stomach pushes through the gap in the diaphragm	I. Hiatal hernia
F	60. Lower left border of stomach	J. Lesser curvature

▶ *If you had difficulty with this section, review pages 485-490.*

SMALL INTESTINE

LIVER AND GALLBLADDER

PANCREAS

Circle the correct answer.

61. Which one is *not* part of the small intestine?
    A. Jejunum
    B. Ileum
    C. Cecum
    D. Duodenum

62. Which one of the following structures does *not* increase the surface area of the intestine for absorption?
    A. Plicae
    B. Rugae
    C. Villi
    D. Brush border

63. The union of the cystic duct and hepatic duct form the:
    A. Common bile duct
    B. Major duodenal papilla
    C. Minor duodenal papilla
    D. Pancreatic duct

64. Obstruction of the _____ will lead to jaundice.
    A. Hepatic duct
    B. Pancreatic duct
    C. Cystic duct
    D. None of the above

65. Bile is responsible for the:
    A. Final digestion of fats
    B. Emulsification of fats
    C. Chemical breakdown of fats
    D. Chemical breakdown of cholesterol

66. The middle third of the duodenum contains the:
    A. Islets
    B. Fundus
    C. Body
    D. Rugae
    E. Major duodenal papilla

67. Cholelithiasis is the term used to describe:
    A. Biliary colic
    B. Jaundice
    C. Portal hypertension
    D. Gallstones

68. The liver is an:
    A. Enzyme
    B. Endocrine organ
    C. Endocrine gland
    D. Exocrine gland

69. Fats in chyme stimulate the secretion of the hormone:
    A. Lipase
    B. Cholecystokinin
    C. Protease
    D. Amylase

70. The largest gland in the body is the:
    A. Pituitary
    B. Thyroid
    C. Liver
    D. Thymus

▷ *If you had difficulty with this section, review pages 490-496.*

LARGE INTESTINE

APPENDIX

PERITONEUM

True or False

If the statement is true, write "T" in the answer blank. If the statement is false, correct the statement by circling the incorrect term and writing the correct term in the answer blank.

__F; vitamin K__ 71. Bacteria in the large intestine are responsible for the synthesis of vitamin E needed for normal blood clotting.

__F; no villi are present__ 72. Villi in the large intestine absorb salts and water.

_____F; diarrhea_____ 73. If waste products pass rapidly through the large intestine, constipation results.

_____F; cecum_____ 74. The ileocecal valve opens into the sigmoid colon.

_____F; hepatic_____ 75. The splenic flexure is the bend between the ascending colon and the transverse colon.

_____F; sigmoid_____ 76. The splenic colon is the S-shaped segment that terminates in the rectum.

_____True_____ 77. The appendix serves no important digestive function in humans.

_____True_____ 78. Appendicitis is more common in children and young adults because the lumen of the appendix is larger during that period making it easier for food and fecal material to become trapped.

_____F; parietal_____ 79. The visceral layer of the peritoneum lines the abdominal cavity.

_____F; mesentery_____ 80. The greater omentum is shaped like a fan and serves to anchor the small intestine to the posterior abdominal wall.

_____F; Diverticulitis_____ 81. Diarrhea is an inflammation of abnormal saclike outpouchings of the intestinal wall.

_____True_____ 82. Crohn disease is a type of autoimmune colitis.

_____True_____ 83. A colostomy is a surgical procedure in which an artificial anus is created on the abdominal wall.

_____F; Ascites_____ 84. Peritonitis is the abnormal accumulation of fluid in the peritoneal space.

▶ *If you had difficulty with this section, review pages 496-500.*

DIGESTION

ABSORPTION

Circle the correct answer.

85. Which one of the following substances does *not* contain any enzymes?
    A. Saliva ✓
    B. Bile
    C. Gastric juice ✓
    D. Pancreatic juice ✓
    E. Intestinal juice ✓

86. Which one of the following is a simple sugar?
    A. Maltose
    B. Sucrose
    C. Lactose
    D. Glucose
    E. Starch

87. Cane sugar is the same as:
    A. Maltose
    B. Lactose
    C. Sucrose
    D. Glucose
    E. None of the above

88. Most of the digestion of carbohydrates takes place in the:
    A. Mouth
    B. Stomach
    C. Small intestine
    D. Large intestine

89. Fats are broken down into:
    A. Amino acids
    B. Simple sugars
    C. Fatty acids
    D. Disaccharides

▶ *If you had difficulty with this section, review pages 500-503.*

CHEMICAL DIGESTION

90. Fill in the blank areas on the chart below.

DIGESTIVE JUICES AND ENZYMES	SUBSTANCE DIGESTED (OR HYDROLYZED)	RESULTING PRODUCT
Saliva		
1. Amylase	1.	1. Maltose
Gastric Juice		
2. Protease (pepsin) plus hydrochloric acid	2. Proteins	2.
Pancreatic Juice		
3. Protease (trypsin)	3. Proteins (intact or partially digested)	3.
4. Lipase	4.	4. Fatty acids, monoglycerides, and glycerol
5. Amylase	5.	5. Maltose
Intestinal Juice		
6. Peptidases	6.	6. Amino acids
7.	7. Sucrose	7. Glucose and fructose
8. Lactase	8.	8. Glucose and galactose (simple sugars)
9. Maltase	9. Maltose	9.

▶ *If you had difficulty with this section, review page 502.*

UNSCRAMBLE THE WORDS

91. **SLBOU**

92. **EYCHM**

93. **LLAAPPI**

94. **PMERTEUION**

Take the circled letters, unscramble them, and fill in the solution.

What the groom gave his bride after the wedding.

95.

APPLYING WHAT YOU KNOW

96. Mr. Amoto is a successful businessman, but he works too hard and is always under great stress. He takes high doses of aspirin, almost daily, to relieve his stress headaches. His doctor cautioned him that if he did not alter his style of living, he would be subject to hyperacidity. What could be a result of hyperacidity?

97. Baby Nicholas has been regurgitating his bottle feeding at every meal. The milk is curdled, but does not appear to be digested. He has become dehydrated, so his mother, Bobbi, is taking him to the pediatrician. What would you guess is a possible diagnosis, based on what you have learned from your textbook reading?

98. Mr. Lynch has high cholesterol. In an effort to lower his cholesterol, he quickly lost 25 pounds by consuming an ultra-low-fat diet. Since then he has noticed a yellowish cast to his skin and has periodic pain in the right upper quadrant of the abdominopelvic region. What is a possible diagnosis for Mr. Lynch? What is the name of the surgical procedure that may be performed on Mr. Lynch?

99. Word Find

Find and circle 22 terms presented in this chapter. Words may be spelled top to bottom, bottom to top, right to left, left to right, or diagonally.

Absorption	Heartburn
Appendix	Jaundice
Cavity	Mastication
Crown	Mesentery
Dentin	Metabolism
Diarrhea	Mucosa
Digestion	Pancreas
Duodenum	Papillae
Emulsify	Peristalsis
Feces	Stomach
Fundus	Uvula

```
X  M  E  T  A  B  O  L  I  S  M  X  X  W
R  S  D  P  E  R  I  S  T  A  L  S  I  S
E  V  A  M  N  O  I  T  S  E  G  I  D  R
E  D  E  E  U  O  Q  T  W  Q  O  H  N  Q
Q  Z  H  S  R  N  I  N  T  F  E  C  E  S
D  H  R  E  C  C  I  T  K  C  J  A  P  E
Q  W  R  N  A  T  N  V  P  Y  R  M  P  C
O  C  A  T  N  R  B  A  P  R  H  O  A  I
U  Y  I  E  O  W  T  A  P  A  O  T  W  D
B  O  D  R  L  N  P  B  F  Q  J  S  V  N
N  T  S  Y  F  I  S  L  U  M  E  E  B  U
W  G  J  A  L  U  V  U  N  R  N  W  O  A
Q  S  N  L  X  D  U  O  D  E  N  U  M  J
H  C  A  V  I  T  Y  M  U  C  O  S  A  D
Y  E  A  A  P  H  V  W  S  V  C  Q  J  C
```

DID YOU KNOW?

- The liver performs over 500 functions and produces over 1000 enzymes to handle the chemical conversions necessary for survival.
- About 20% of older adults have diabetes, and almost 40% have some impaired glucose tolerance.
- The human stomach lining replaces itself every 3 days.

KNOW YOUR MEDICAL TERMS

Fill in the medical term from the literal translation.

100. Lump _____

101. Blind or hidden/thing _____

102. Break apart/process _____

103. Waste _____

104. Chew/process _____

105. Roof of mouth _____

106. Wrinkle _____

107. Worm/shape/hang upon/thing _____

108. Yellow/state _____

109. Decay _____

110. Large intestine/see/activity _____

▷ *If you had difficulty with this section, review pages 476-479.*

DIGESTIVE SYSTEM

Fill in the crossword puzzle.

ACROSS

5. Digested food moves from intestine to blood
8. Semisolid mixture
9. Inflammation of the appendix
11. Rounded mass of food
13. Stomach folds

DOWN

1. Yellowish skin discoloration
2. Process of chewing
3. Fluid stools
4. Movement of food through digestive tract
6. Vomitus
7. Waste product of digestion
10. Intestinal fold
12. Open wound in digestive area acted on by acid juices
14. Prevents food from entering nasal cavities

CHECK YOUR KNOWLEDGE

Multiple Choice

Circle the correct answer.

1. During the process of digestion, *stored* bile is poured into the duodenum by which of the following?
   A. Gallbladder
   B. Liver
   C. Pancreas
   D. Spleen

2. Which portion of the alimentary canal mixes food with gastric juice and breaks it down into a mixture called *chyme*?
   A. Gallbladder
   B. Small intestine
   C. Stomach
   D. Large intestine

3. What is the middle portion of the small intestine called?
   A. Jejunum
   B. Ileum
   C. Duodenum
   D. Cecum

4. The crown of the tooth is covered externally with which of the following?
   A. Cementum
   B. Enamel
   C. Dentin
   D. Pulp

5. What is the layer of tissue that forms the outermost covering of organs found in the digestive tract called?
   A. Mucosa
   B. Serosa
   C. Submucosa
   D. Muscularis

6. Duodenal ulcers appear in which of the following?
   A. Stomach
   B. Small intestine
   C. Large intestine
   D. Esophagus

7. What is an extension of the peritoneum that is shaped like a giant pleated fan?
   A. Omentum
   B. Mesentery
   C. Peritoneal cavity
   D. Ligament

8. Protein digestion begins in the:
   A. Esophagus
   B. Small intestine
   C. Stomach
   D. Large intestine

9. The enzyme pepsin is concerned primarily with the digestion of which of the following?
   A. Sugars
   B. Starches
   C. Proteins
   D. Fats

10. The enzyme amylase converts which of the following?
    A. Starches to sugars
    B. Sugars to starches
    C. Proteins to amino acids
    D. Fatty acids and glycerol to fats

Completion

Fill in the blanks using the terms listed below. Write the corresponding letter in each blank. Not all letters will be used.

A. Ileum	G. Lower esophageal sphincter	M. Upper esophageal sphincter	S. Premolars
B. Amylase	H. Digestion	N. Sigmoid colon	T. Mucosa
C. Muscularis	I. Incisors	O. Canines	U. Submucosa
D. Metabolism	J. Greater omentum	P. Amino acids	V. Cecum
E. Cholecystokinin	K. Absorption	Q. Duodenum	W. Bile
F. Molars	L. Adventitia	R. Jejunum	X. Serosa

11. The S-shaped portion of the colon is called the _____.

12. The portion of the peritoneum that descends from the stomach and the transverse colon to form a lacy apron of fat over the intestines is called the _____.

13. The "building blocks" of protein molecules are _____.

14. The small intestine is made up of three sections called the _____, _____, and the _____.

15. Fats that enter into the digestive tract are emulsified when they are acted on by a substance called _____.

16. Foods undergo three kinds of processing in the body: _____, _____, and _____.

17. Fats in the chyme stimulate the secretion of _____, which stimulates contraction of the gallbladder to release bile.

18. The four tissue layers that make up the wall of the digestive tract are the _____, _____, _____, and _____.

19. Food enters the stomach by passing through a muscular structure at the end of the esophagus. This structure is called the _____.

20. The four major types of teeth found in the human mouth are _____, _____, _____, and _____.

LOCATION OF DIGESTIVE ORGANS

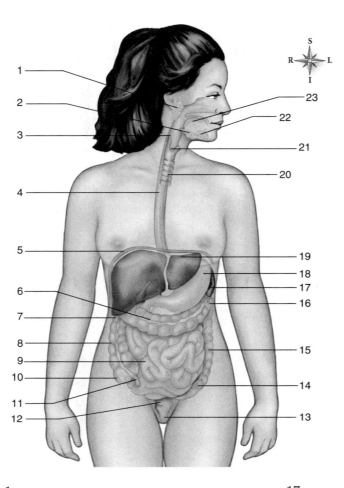

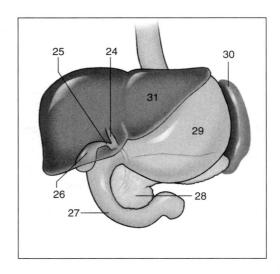

1. _____	17. _____
2. _____	18. _____
3. _____	19. _____
4. _____	20. _____
5. _____	21. _____
6. _____	22. _____
7. _____	23. _____
8. _____	24. _____
9. _____	25. _____
10. _____	26. _____
11. _____	27. _____
12. _____	28. _____
13. _____	29. _____
14. _____	30. _____
15. _____	31. _____
16. _____	

TOOTH

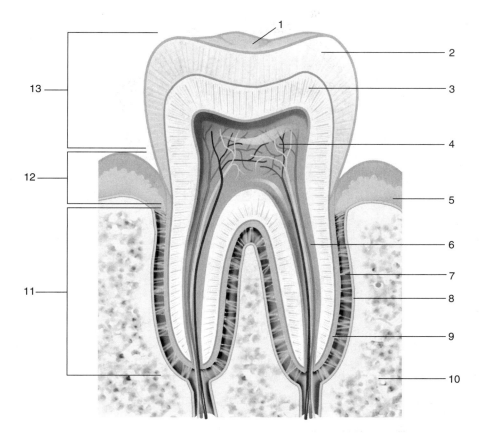

1. _____

2. _____

3. _____

4. _____

5. _____

6. _____

7. _____

8. _____

9. _____

10. _____

11. _____

12. _____

13. _____

THE SALIVARY GLANDS

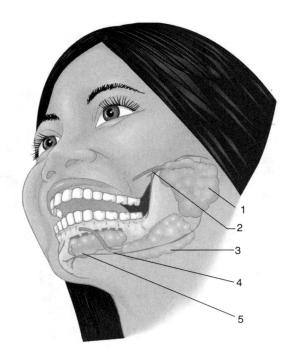

1. _____

2. _____

3. _____

4. _____

5. _____

STOMACH

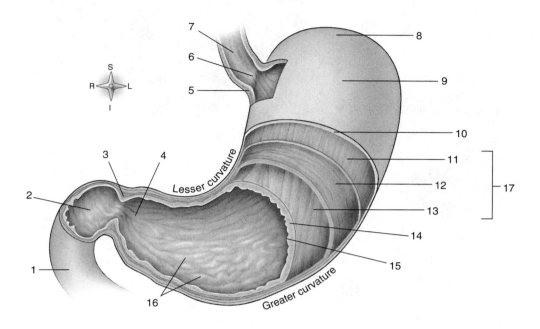

1. _____

2. _____

3. _____

4. _____

5. _____

6. _____

7. _____

8. _____

9. _____

10. _____

11. _____

12. _____

13. _____

14. _____

15. _____

16. _____

17. _____

GALLBLADDER AND BILE DUCTS

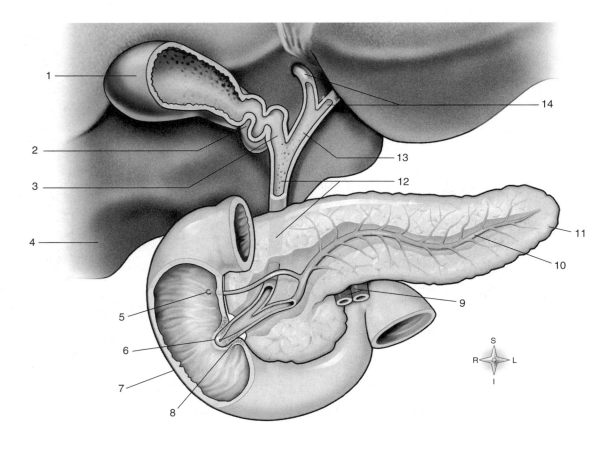

1. _____   8. _____

2. _____   9. _____

3. _____   10. _____

4. _____   11. _____

5. _____   12. _____

6. _____   13. _____

7. _____   14. _____

THE SMALL INTESTINE

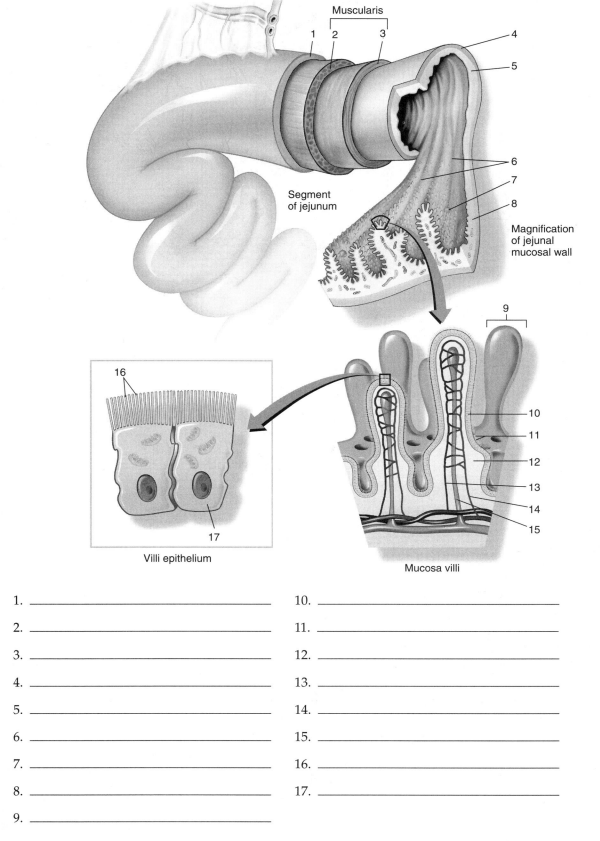

Muscularis

Segment
of jejunum

Magnification
of jejunal
mucosal wall

Villi epithelium

Mucosa villi

1. _____

2. _____

3. _____

4. _____

5. _____

6. _____

7. _____

8. _____

9. _____

10. _____

11. _____

12. _____

13. _____

14. _____

15. _____

16. _____

17. _____

THE LARGE INTESTINE

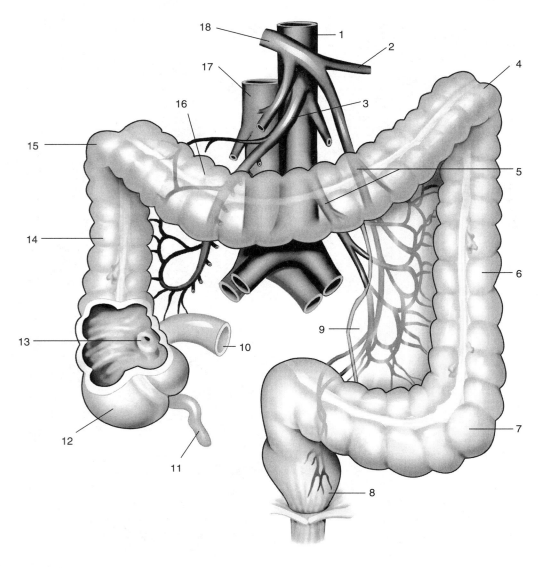

1. _____

2. _____

3. _____

4. _____

5. _____

6. _____

7. _____

8. _____

9. _____

10. _____

11. _____

12. _____

13. _____

14. _____

15. _____

16. _____

17. _____

18. _____

CHAPTER 19

Nutrition and Metabolism

Most of us love to eat, but do the foods we enjoy provide us with the basic food types necessary for good nutrition? The body, a finely tuned machine, requires a balance of carbohydrates, fats, proteins, vitamins, and minerals to function properly. These nutrients must be digested, absorbed, and circulated to cells constantly to accommodate the numerous activities that occur throughout the body. The use the body makes of foods once these processes are completed is called *metabolism*.

The liver plays a major role in the metabolism of food. It helps maintain a normal blood glucose level, removes toxins from the blood, processes blood immediately after it leaves the gastrointestinal tract, and initiates the first steps of protein and fat metabolism.

This chapter also discusses basal metabolic rate (BMR). The BMR is the rate at which food is catabolized under basal conditions. This test and the protein-bound iodine (PBI) are indirect measures of thyroid gland functioning. The total metabolic rate (TMR) is the amount of energy, expressed in calories, used by the body each day.

Finally, maintaining a constant body temperature is a function of the hypothalamus and a challenge for the metabolic mechanisms of the body. Review of this chapter is necessary to provide you with an understanding of the "fuel" (nutrition) requirements necessary to maintain this complex homeostatic machine—the body.

TOPICS FOR REVIEW

Before progressing to Chapter 20, you should be able to define and contrast catabolism and anabolism. Your review should include the metabolic roles of carbohydrates, fats, proteins, vitamins, and minerals. Your study should conclude with an understanding of the basal metabolic rate, physiological mechanisms that regulate body temperature, and the common metabolic and eating disorders.

METABOLIC FUNCTIONS OF THE LIVER

Fill in the blanks.

The liver plays an important role in the mechanical digestion of lipids because it secretes

(1) _____. It also produces two of the plasma proteins that play an essential role in blood clotting. These two proteins are

(2) _____ and (3) _____.
Additionally, liver cells store several substances, notably vitamins A and D and

(4) _____. Finally, the liver is assisted by a unique structural feature of the blood vessels that supply it. This arrangement, known as the

(5) _____ _____

_____, allows toxins to be removed from the bloodstream before nutrients are distributed throughout the body.

NUTRIENT METABOLISM

Match each term with its corresponding definition. (Answers may be used more than once.)

_____ 6. Used if cells have inadequate amounts of glucose to catabolize

_____ 7. Preferred energy food

_____ 8. Amino acids

_____ 9. Fat soluble

_____ 10. Required for nerve conduction

_____ 11. Glycolysis

_____ 12. Inorganic elements found naturally in the earth

_____ 13. Pyruvic acid

A. Carbohydrate

B. Fat

C. Protein

D. Vitamins

E. Minerals

Circle the term in each word group that does not belong.

14. Glycolysis	Citric acid cycle	ATP	Bile
15. Adipose	Amino acids	Triglycerides	Lipid
16. A	D	M	K
17. Iron	Proteins	Amino acids	Essential
18. Hydrocortisone	Insulin	Growth hormone	Epinephrine
19. Sodium	Calcium	Zinc	Folic acid
20. Thiamine	Niacin	Ascorbic acid	Riboflavin

▷ *If you had difficulty with this section, review pages 511-518.*

METABOLIC RATES

Circle the correct answer.

21. The rate at which food is catabolized under basal conditions is the:
    A. TMR
    B. PBI
    C. BMR
    D. ATP

22. The total amount of energy used by the body per day is the:
    A. TMR
    B. PBI
    C. BMR
    D. ATP

23. A/an _____ is the amount of energy needed to raise the temperature of 1 gram of water 1° Celsius.
    A. Calorie
    B. Kilocalorie
    C. ATP
    D. BMR

24. Which of the following is a factor when determining the BMR?
    A. Sex
    B. Age
    C. Size
    D. All of the above

25. Which of the following is a factor when determining the TMR?
    A. Exercise
    B. Food intake
    C. Environmental temperature
    D. All of the above

▷ *If you had difficulty with this section, review pages 518-520.*

METABOLIC AND EATING DISORDERS

Match each description with its related term. Write the corresponding letter in the answer blank.

_____ 26. Insulin deficiency is a symptom of this disorder

_____ 27. Behavioral disorder characterized by chronic refusal to eat

_____ 28. An advanced form of PCM

_____ 29. Results from a deficiency of calories in general and protein in particular

_____ 30. Hypothyroidism will affect this measurement

_____ 31. Abdominal bloating

_____ 32. Symptom of chronic overeating behavior

_____ 33. Behavioral disorder characterized by insatiable craving for food alternating with periods of self-deprivation

A. BMR

B. Diabetes mellitus

C. Anorexia nervosa

D. Bulimia

E. Obesity

F. PCM

G. Marasmus

H. Ascites

▷ *If you had difficulty with this section, review pages 520-521.*

BODY TEMPERATURES

Circle the correct answer.

34. Over _____ of the energy released from food molecules during catabolism is converted to heat rather than being transferred to ATP.
    A. 20%
    B. 40%
    C. 60%
    D. 80%

35. Maintaining thermoregulation is a function of the:
    A. Thalamus
    B. Hypothalamus
    C. Thyroid
    D. Parathyroids

36. Transfer of heat energy to the skin, then the external environment is known as:
    A. Radiation
    B. Conduction
    C. Convection
    D. Evaporation

37. A flow of heat waves away from the blood is known as:
    A. Radiation
    B. Conduction
    C. Convection
    D. Evaporation

38. A transfer of heat energy to air that is continually flowing away from the skin is known as:
    A. Radiation
    B. Conduction
    C. Convection
    D. Evaporation

39. Heat that is absorbed by the process of water vaporization is called:
    A. Radiation
    B. Conduction
    C. Convection
    D. Evaporation

▷ *If you had difficulty with this section, review pages 521-522.*

ABNORMAL BODY TEMPERATURE

True or False

If the statement is true, write "T" in the answer blank. If the statement is false, correct the statement by circling the incorrect term and writing the correct term in the answer blank.

_____ 40. Pyrogens cause the thermostatic control centers of the hypothalamus to produce a fever.

_____ 41. Malignant hyperthermia is the inability to maintain a normal body temperature in extremely cold environments.

_____ 42. Frostbite is local damage to tissues caused by extremely low temperatures.

_____ 43. Heat exhaustion is characterized by body temperatures of 41° Celsius or higher.

_____ 44. Dantrium is used to prevent or relieve the effects of frostbite.

▷ *If you had difficulty with this section, review pages 522-524.*

UNSCRAMBLE THE WORDS

45. **L R I E V**

46. **T A O B A L I C M S**

47. **O M N I A**

48. **Y P U R C V I**

Take the circled letters, unscramble them, and fill in the solution.

How the magician paid his bills.

49.

APPLYING WHAT YOU KNOW

50. Dr. Carey is concerned about Deborah. Her daily food intake provides fewer calories than her TMR. If this trend continues, what will be the result? If it continues over a long time, what eating disorder might Deborah develop?

51. Kathryn has been experiencing fatigue, and a blood test reveals that she is slightly anemic. What mineral will her doctor most likely prescribe? What dietary sources might you suggest that she emphasize in her daily intake?

52. Joe is training daily for an upcoming marathon. Three days before the 25-mile event, he suddenly quits his daily routine of jogging and switches to a diet high in carbohydrates. Why did Joe suddenly switch his routine of training?

53. Word Find

Find and circle 18 terms presented in this chapter. Words may be spelled top to bottom, bottom to top, right to left, left to right, or diagonally.

ATP
Adipose
BMR
Bile
Carbohydrates
Catabolism
Conduction
Convection
Evaporation
Fats
Glycerol
Glycolysis
Liver
Minerals
Proteins
Radiation
TMR
Vitamins

```
C  C  C  B  W  E  F  F  L  J  V  G  G  S
A  T  N  L  W  E  U  O  Z  I  E  L  I  B
R  K  K  P  Z  F  R  I  T  P  O  Y  K  L
B  Q  M  I  N  E  R  A  L  S  J  C  C  P
O  S  S  N  C  X  M  I  D  B  D  O  W  P
H  S  I  Y  O  I  T  X  H  I  N  L  S  N
Y  E  L  N  N  I  K  W  W  D  S  Y  N  S
D  G  O  S  O  W  T  I  U  E  H  S  C  N
R  M  B  Y  T  I  W  C  Z  N  N  I  A  A
A  R  A  Q  W  A  T  B  E  I  G  S  J  M
T  E  T  F  N  I  F  A  E  V  E  W  T  Y
E  V  A  P  O  R  A  T  I  O  N  D  T  E
S  I  C  N  E  S  O  P  I  D  A  O  F  E
H  L  Y  K  I  R  E  B  V  P  A  H  C  J
I  W  E  E  P  A  D  F  T  E  A  R  G  G
```

KNOW YOUR MEDICAL TERMS

Fill in the complete words in the spaces provided for these abbreviations.

54. BMR _____

55. ETS _____

56. TMR _____

57. PCM _____

58. ATP _____

59. F _____

60. K _____

▶ *If you had difficulty with this section, review pages 512-519.*

DID YOU KNOW?

- The amount of energy required for a person to raise a 200-pound man 15 feet in the air is about the amount of energy in one large calorie.

NUTRITION/METABOLISM

Fill in the crossword puzzle.

ACROSS

1. Breaks food molecules down, releasing stored energy
4. Amount of energy needed to raise the temperature of 1 gram of water 1° Celsius
7. Rate of metabolism when a person is lying down, but awake (abbreviation)
8. A series of reactions that join glucose molecules together to form glycogen
10. Builds food molecules into complex substances

DOWN

2. Occurs when food molecules enter cells and undergo many chemical changes there
3. Organic molecule needed in small quantities for normal metabolism throughout the body
5. Oxygen-using
6. A unit of measure for heat, also known as a large calorie
9. Takes place in the cytoplasm of a cell and changes glucose to pyruvic acid

CHECK YOUR KNOWLEDGE

Multiple Choice

Circle the correct answer.

1. The citric acid cycle changes acetyl CoA to:
   A. Oxygen
   B. Carbon dioxide
   C. Pyruvic acid
   D. Glucose

2. The anabolism of glucose produces which of the following?
   A. Glycogen
   B. Amino acid
   C. Rennin
   D. Starch

3. Which of the following is a major hormone in the body that aids carbohydrate metabolism?
   A. Oxytocin
   B. Epinephrine
   C. Insulin
   D. Growth hormone

4. The total metabolic rate is which of the following?
   A. The amount of fats a person consumes in a 24-hour period
   B. The same as the BMR
   C. The amount of energy expressed in calories used by the body per day
   D. Cannot be calculated

5. When your consumption of calories equals your TMR, your weight will do which of the following?
   A. Increase
   B. Remain the same
   C. Fluctuate
   D. Decrease

6. Which of the following is a normal glucose level?
   A. 40 to 80 mg/100 ml blood
   B. 80 to 120 mg/100 ml blood
   C. 100 to 140 mg/100 ml blood
   D. 180 to 220 mg/100 ml blood

7. When glucose is *not* available, the body will next catabolize which of the following energy sources?
   A. Fats
   B. Proteins
   C. Minerals
   D. Vitamins

8. Maintaining the homeostasis of the body temperature is the responsibility of which of the following?
   A. Hypothalamus
   B. Environmental condition in which we live
   C. Circulatory system
   D. None of the above

9. The liver plays an important role in the mechanical digestion of lipids because it secretes:
   A. Glucose molecules
   B. Bile
   C. Glycogen
   D. Citric acid

10. What is the primary molecule the body usually breaks down as an energy source?
    A. Amino acid
    B. Pepsin
    C. Maltose
    D. Glucose

Completion

Complete the following statements using the terms listed below. Write the corresponding letter in the answer blank.

A. Vitamins   H. Sodium

B. Insulin   I. Proteins

C. Carbohydrates   J. Citric acid cycle

D. Fats   K. Calcium

E. Glycolysis   L. Glycogen loading

F. Metabolism   M. Triglycerides

G. ATP

11. Proper nutrition requires the balance of the three basic food types: _____, _____, and _____.

12. The process that changes glucose to pyruvic acid is called _____.

13. Once glucose has been changed to pyruvic acid, another process in which pyruvic acid is changed to carbon dioxide takes place. This reaction is known as the _____.

14. A direct source of energy for doing cellular work is _____.

15. The only hormone that lowers blood glucose level is _____.

16. Fats not needed for catabolism are anabolized to form _____.

17. Some athletes consume large amounts of carbohydrates 2 to 3 days before an athletic event to store glycogen in skeletal muscles. This practice is called _____.

18. Organic molecules needed in small amounts for normal metabolism are _____.

19. Two minerals necessary for nerve conduction and contraction of muscle fibers are _____ and _____.

20. The "use of nutrients" is known as _____.

CHAPTER 20

The Urinary System

L iving produces wastes. Wherever people live, work, or play, wastes accumulate. To keep these areas healthy, there must be a method of disposing of these wastes such as the services provided by a sanitation department. Wastes also accumulate in your body. The conversion of food and gases into substances and energy necessary for survival results in waste products. A large percentage of these wastes is removed by the urinary system.

Two vital organs, the kidneys, cleanse the blood of the many waste products that are continually produced as a result of the metabolism of nutrients taken into the body cells. They eliminate these wastes in the form of urine.

Urine formation is the result of three processes: filtration, reabsorption, and secretion. These processes occur in successive portions of the microscopic units of the kidneys known as *nephrons*. The amount of urine produced by the nephrons is controlled primarily by the hormones ADH and aldosterone.

After urine is produced, it is drained from the renal pelvis by the ureters to flow into the bladder. The bladder then stores the urine until it is voided through the urethra.

If waste products are allowed to accumulate in the body, they soon become poisonous, a condition called *uremia*. A knowledge of the urinary system is necessary to understand how the body rids itself of waste and avoids toxicity.

TOPICS FOR REVIEW

Before progressing to Chapter 21, you should have an understanding of the structure and function of the organs of the urinary system. Your review should include knowledge of the nephron and its role in urine production. Your study should conclude with a review of the three main processes involved in urine production, the mechanisms that control urine volume, and the major renal and urinary disorders.

KIDNEYS

KIDNEY FUNCTION

Circle the correct answer.

1. The outermost portion of the kidney is known as the:
   A. Medulla
   B. Papilla
   C. Pelvis
   D. Pyramid
   E. Cortex

2. The saclike structure that surrounds the glomerulus is the:
   A. Renal pelvis
   B. Calyx
   C. Bowman capsule
   D. Cortex
   E. None of the above

3. The renal corpuscle is made up of the:
   A. Bowman capsule and proximal convoluted tubule
   B. Glomerulus and proximal convoluted tubule
   C. Bowman capsule and the distal convoluted tubule
   D. Glomerulus and the distal convoluted tubule
   E. Bowman capsule and the glomerulus

4. Which of the following functions is *not* performed by the kidneys?
   A. Help maintain homeostasis
   B. Remove wastes from the blood
   C. Produce ADH
   D. Remove electrolytes from the blood

Match each descriptive phrase with its related structure. Write the corresponding letter in the answer blank.

___G___ 5. Functioning unit of the urinary system

___K___ 6. Together with the Bowman capsule forms the renal corpuscle

___F___ 7. Division of the renal pelvis

___H___ 8. Straight part of renal tubule

___D___ 9. Innermost end of a pyramid

___L___ 10. Extension of the proximal tubule

___C___ 11. Triangular-shaped divisions of the medulla of the kidney

___E___ 12. An expansion of the upper end of a ureter

___A___ 13. Inner portion of the kidney

___J___ 14. Toxic level of waste products in the blood

___I___ 15. Cells secrete an enzyme that assists in restoring normal blood pressure and blood volume

___M___ 16. Hormone secreted by kidney

___B___ 17. Outer portion of kidney

A. Medulla
B. Cortex
C. Pyramids
D. Papilla
E. Pelvis
F. Calyx
G. Nephron
H. Collecting duct
I. Juxtaglomerular apparatus (JG)
J. Uremia
K. Glomerulus
L. Henle loop
M. Erythropoietin

▷ *If you had difficulty with this section, review pages 528-536.*

URETERS

URINARY BLADDER

URETHRA

Match each descriptive phrase with its related structure and write the corresponding letter in the answer blank.

A. Ureters   B. Bladder   C. Urethra

_C_ 18. Lies between the urinary meatus and bladder

_B_ 19. Rugae

_C_ 20. Lowest part of the urinary tract

_A_ 21. Lining membrane richly supplied with sensory nerve endings

_B_ 22. Lies behind the pubic symphysis

_C_ 23. Serves a dual function in the male

_C_ 24. 1½ inches long in the female

_A_ 25. Drain the renal pelvis

_C_ 26. Surrounded by the prostate in the male

_B_ 27. Consists of elastic fibers and involuntary muscle fibers

_A_ 28. 10 to 12 inches long

_B_ 29. Trigone

▶ *If you had difficulty with this section, review pages 536-538.*

MICTURITION

Fill in the blanks.

The terms (30) _micturition_, (31) _urination_, and
(32) _voiding_ all refer to the passage of urine from the body or the emptying
of the bladder. The sphincters guard the bladder. The (33) _internal_
urethral _sphincter_ is the sphincter located
at the bladder (34) _exit_ and is involuntary. The external urethral
sphincter encircles the (35) _urethra_ and is under
(36) _voluntary_ control. As the bladder fills, nervous impulses are transmitted
to the spinal cord and an (37) _emptying reflex_ is initiated. Urine then enters the
(38) _urethra_ to be eliminated. Urinary
(39) _retention_ is a condition in which no urine is voided. Urinary
(40) _suppression_ is when the kidneys do not produce any urine, but the bladder
retains its ability to empty itself. The term (41) _Stress_
incontinence is often used to describe the type of urine loss associated with
laughing, coughing, or heavy lifting.

▶ *If you had difficulty with this section, review pages 538-539.*

RENAL PHYSIOLOGY

CONTROL OF URINE VOLUME

URINALYSIS

Circle the correct answer.

42. _____ % of the glomerular filtrate is reabsorbed.
    A. 20
    B. 40
    C. 75
    D. 85
    E. 99 *(circled)*

43. The glomerular filtration rate is _____ ml per minute.
    A. 1.25
    B. 12.5
    C. 125.0 *(circled)*
    D. 1250.0
    E. None of the above

44. Glucose reabsorption begins in the:
    A. Henle loop
    B. Proximal convoluted tubule *(circled)*
    C. Distal convoluted tubule
    D. Glomerulus
    E. None of the above

45. Reabsorption does *not* occur in the:
    A. Henle loop ✓
    B. Proximal convoluted tubule ✓
    C. Distal convoluted tubule ✓
    D. Collecting duct ✓
    E. Calyx *(circled)*

46. The greater the amount of salt intake, the:
    A. Less salt is excreted in the urine
    B. More salt is reabsorbed
    C. More salt is excreted in the urine *(circled)*
    D. None of the above

47. Which one of the following substances is secreted by diffusion?
    A. Sodium ions
    B. Certain drugs
    C. Ammonia
    D. Hydrogen ions
    E. Potassium ions

48. Which of the following statements about ADH is *not* correct?
    A. It is stored by the pituitary gland.
    B. It makes the collecting ducts less permeable to water. ✓
    C. It makes the distal convoluted tubules more permeable. — *(circled)*
    D. It is produced by the hypothalamus.

49. Which of the following statements about aldosterone is *not* correct?
    A. It is secreted by the adrenal cortex. ✓
    B. It is a water-retaining hormone. ✓
    C. It is a salt-retaining hormone. ✓
    D. All of the above are correct. *(circled)*

Fill in the blanks.

50. The physical, chemical, and microscopic examination of urine is termed _urinalysis_.

51. A standard urinalysis is often referred to as a _routine_ _and_ _microscopic_.

52. Urine specimens are often spun in a _centrifuge_ to force suspended particles to the bottom of a test tube.

53. Small particles that are often formed by minerals and that may break off in the urine are known as _casts_.

54. Clinical studies have proven that improper catheterization techniques cause _bladder infections_ in hospitalized patients.

55. Changes in specific gravity may be due to insufficient _fluid_ intake.

▶ *If you had difficulty with this section, review pages 539-543.*

RENAL AND URINARY DISORDERS

Match each descriptive phrase with its related disorder. Write the corresponding letter in the answer blank.

_I_ 56. Urine backs up into the kidneys causing swelling of the renal pelvis and calyces

_C_ 57. Kidney stones develop

_G_ 58. Stage 2 of chronic renal failure

_F_ 59. Blood in the urine

_K_ 60. Inflammation of the bladder

_A_ 61. Inflammation of the renal pelvis and connective tissues of the kidney

_H_ 62. An abrupt reduction in kidney function characterized by oliguria and a sharp rise in nitrogenous compounds in the blood

_J_ 63. Progressive condition resulting from gradual loss of nephrons

_B_ 64. Intense kidney pain caused by obstruction of the ureters by large kidney stones

_D_ 65. Most common form of kidney disease caused by a delayed immune response to streptococcal infection

_E_ 66. Albumin in the urine

_L_ 67. Inflammation of the urethra that commonly results from bacterial infection

A. Pyelonephritis
B. Renal colic
C. Renal calculi
D. Acute glomerulonephritis
E. Proteinuria
F. Hematuria
G. Renal insufficiency
H. Acute renal failure
I. Hydronephrosis
J. Chronic renal failure
K. Cystitis
L. Urethritis

▶ *If you had difficulty with this section, review pages 543-550.*

UNSCRAMBLE THE WORDS

68. **A Y X L C**

☐☐☐☐⊙☐

69. **G V N O I D I**

☐☐☐⊙⊙☐☐

70. **A L P A L I P**

☐☐⊙☐☐☐⊙

71. **S G U L L O U M R E**

☐☐☐☐⊙☐⊙☐☐☐⊙

Take the circled letters, unscramble them, and fill in the solution.

What Betty saw while cruising down the Nile.

72. ☐☐☐☐☐☐☐☐☐

APPLYING WHAT YOU KNOW

73. John suffers from low levels of ADH. What primary urinary symptom would he notice?

74. Bud was in a diving accident and his spinal cord was severed. He was paralyzed from the waist down and as a result is incontinent. His physician, Dr. Welch, is concerned about the continuous residual urine buildup. What is the reason for concern?

75. Mrs. Lynch had a prolonged surgical procedure and experienced problems with urinary retention post-operatively. A urinary catheter was inserted into her bladder for the elimination of urine. Several days later Mrs. Lynch developed cystitis. What might be a possible cause of this diagnosis?

76. Mr. Dietz, an accident victim, was admitted to the hospital several hours ago. His chart indicates that he had been hemorrhaging at the scene of the accident. Nurse Petersen has been closely monitoring his urinary output and has noted that it has dropped to 10 ml/hr. (The normal urine output for a healthy adult is approximately 30 to 60 ml/hr.) What might explain this drop in urine output?

77. Word Find

Find and circle 18 terms presented in this chapter. Words may be spelled top to bottom, bottom to top, right to left, left to right, or diagonally.

```
H N O I T I R U T C I M N M Y
V E Q N G A L L I P A P S E S
T P M C O L D U J Y S I N D D
L H G O X I O W C G V D I U J
C R F N D B T M T L I M B K L
P O O T X I C A E K A P X L D
Q N U I E G A P R R T C W A O
B J R N T T L L Y T U Y G D M
S D E E R G Y P Y V L L P H Z
I H T N O U X W D S X I U J G
M X E C C Y S T I T I S F S Q
J O R E D D A L B U E S G B S
Y I S E B V L L B H V Q L U L
```

ADH	Filtration	Micturition
Bladder	Glomerulus	Nephron
Calculi	Hemodialysis	Papilla
Calyx	Incontinence	Pelvis
Cortex	Kidney	Pyramids
Cystitis	Medulla	Ureters

KNOW YOUR MEDICAL TERMS

Identify the medical term from the literal translation.

78. _____ Seed pod or cup

79. _____ Strain/process

80. _____ Urinate/process

81. _____ Backward/around/stretched/relating to

82. _____ Bag/see

83. _____ Kidney/substance

84. _____ Kidney/unit

85. _____ Not/urine/condition

A. Micturition

B. Nephron

C. Calyx

D. Anuria

E. Filtration

F. Cystoscope

G. Retroperitoneal

H. Renin

▶ *If you had difficulty with this section, review pages 530 and 531.*

DID YOU KNOW?

- If the tubules in a kidney were stretched out and untangled, they would measure 70 miles in length.
- One out of every six men will develop prostate cancer in his lifetime, but only one man in every 35 will die from it.
- Half of one kidney could do the work that two kidneys usually do.
- Over 400 gallons of recycled blood is pumped through your kidneys every day.

URINARY SYSTEM

Fill in the crossword puzzle.

ACROSS

3. Bladder infection
7. Absence of urine
8. Passage of a tube into the bladder to withdraw urine
11. Network of blood capillaries tucked into Bowman capsule

DOWN

1. Urination
2. Ultrasound generator used to break up kidney stones
3. Division of the renal pelvis
4. Voiding involuntarily
5. Area on posterior bladder wall free of rugae
6. Glucose in the urine
9. Large amount of urine
10. Scanty urine

CHECK YOUR KNOWLEDGE

Multiple Choice

Circle the correct answer.

1. Which of the following is true of urinary catheterization?
   A. It can be used to treat retention.
   B. It requires aseptic technique.
   C. It can lead to cystitis.
   D. All of the above are true.

2. Which of the following processes are used by the artificial kidney to remove waste materials from blood?
   A. Pinocytosis
   B. Hemodialysis
   C. Catheterization
   D. Active transport

3. Failure of the kidneys to remove wastes from the blood will result in which of the following?
   A. Retention
   B. Anuria
   C. Incontinence
   D. Uremia

4. Hydrogen ions are transferred from blood into the urine during which of the following processes?
   A. Secretion
   B. Filtration
   C. Reabsorption
   D. All of the above

KIDNEY

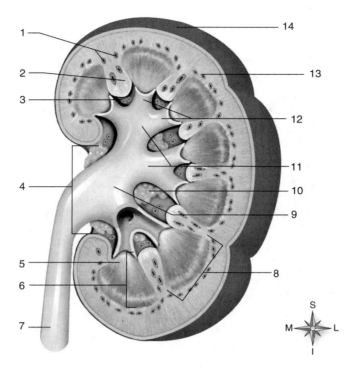

1. _____

2. _____

3. _____

4. _____

5. _____

6. _____

7. _____

8. _____

9. _____

10. _____

11. _____

12. _____

13. _____

14. _____

NEPHRON

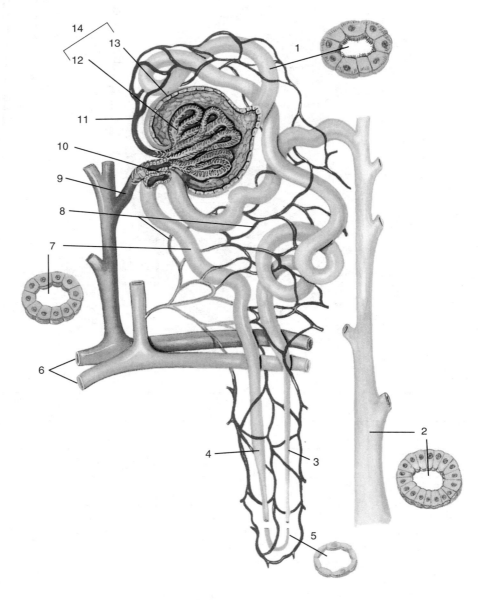

1. _____   8. _____

2. _____   9. _____

3. _____   10. _____

4. _____   11. _____

5. _____   12. _____

6. _____   13. _____

7. _____   14. _____

51. Word Find

Find and circle 12 terms presented in this chapter. Words may be spelled top to bottom, bottom to top, right to left, left to right, or diagonally.

```
S  T  V  H  O  M  E  O  S  T  A  S  I  S  H
I  E  D  E  M  A  S  Q  A  L  P  U  E  G  L
M  M  L  U  F  L  U  I  D  O  Y  O  I  S  L
W  S  B  E  A  E  C  O  L  D  P  N  I  E  R
L  I  T  A  C  V  S  H  Q  O  C  E  H  B  C
L  L  X  J  L  T  E  A  W  Y  B  V  Q  Q  O
I  O  O  P  E  A  R  U  C  T  C  A  A  R  I
N  B  H  R  X  S  N  O  I  I  P  R  T  C  N
S  A  O  X  M  G  J  C  L  N  J  T  B  A  H
I  N  X  X  D  V  U  D  E  Y  K  N  Y  O  C
E  A  A  J  Q  D  I  U  R  E  T  I  C  S  X
I  F  C  J  A  M  P  V  E  N  B  E  Y  F  W
V  F  K  T  Q  X  R  M  D  D  S  I  V  O  T
E  T  T  Z  N  T  R  P  X  I  M  L  J  F  I
S  W  Y  A  P  V  Q  N  S  K  T  K  W  B  P
```

Aldosterone	Edema	Imbalance
Anabolism	Electrolyte	Intravenous
Catabolism	Fluid	Ions
Diuretics	Homeostasis	Kidney

KNOW YOUR MEDICAL TERMS

Select the term that matches the definition.

A. Dissociate   D. Cation   G. Anion

B. Nonelectrolyte   E. Electrolyte   H. Ion

C. Hypernatremia   F. Hyperkalemia   I. Overhydration

52. _____ Positively charged particle

53. _____ Action in which a compound breaks apart in solution

54. _____ Compound that does not dissociate into ions in solution

55. _____ Substance that dissociates into ions in solution

56. _____ Negatively charged particle

57. _____ Elevation of potassium in the blood

58. _____ Too much fluid input in the body

59. _____ Electrically charged atom

60. _____ Elevation of sodium in the blood

▶ *If you had difficulty with this section, review page 558.*

DID YOU KNOW?

- The best fluid replacement drink is 1/4 teaspoon of table salt added to 1 quart of water.
- If all of the water were drained from the body of an average 160-pound man, the body would weigh 64 pounds.

FLUID/ELECTROLYTES

Fill in the crossword puzzle.

ACROSS

3. Result of rapidly given intravenous fluids
4. Result of large loss of body fluids
5. Compound that dissociates in solution into ions
7. To break up
9. A subdivision of extracellular fluid (abbreviation)

DOWN

1. Organic substance that doesn't dissociate in solution
2. Dissociated particles of an electrolyte that carry an electrical charge
5. Fluid outside cells (abbreviation)
6. "Causing urine"
8. Fluid inside cells (abbreviation)

CHECK YOUR KNOWLEDGE

Multiple Choice

Circle the correct answer.

1. Which of the following statements, if any, is *false*?
   A. The more fat present in the body, the more total water content per unit of weight.
   B. The body weight of infants is composed of a higher percentage of water in comparison with the body weight of adults.
   C. As age increases, the amount of water per pound of body weight decreases.
   D. All of the above statements are true.

2. Avenues of fluid output include which of the following?
   A. Skin
   B. Lungs
   C. Kidneys
   D. All of the above

3. Excessive water loss and fluid imbalance can result from which of the following?
   A. Diarrhea
   B. Vomiting
   C. Severe burns
   D. All of the above

4. What factor is primarily responsible for moving water from interstitial fluid into blood?
   A. Aldosterone secretions
   B. Pressure in blood capillaries
   C. Protein concentration of blood plasma
   D. Antidiuretic hormone secretions

5. What is the chief regulator of sodium levels in body fluids?
   A. Kidney
   B. Intestine
   C. Blood
   D. Lung

6. If blood sodium concentration decreases, what is the effect on blood volume?
   A. Increases
   B. Decreases
   C. Remains the same
   D. None of the above

7. Which of the following is true of body water?
   A. It is obtained from the liquids we drink.
   B. It is obtained from the foods we eat.
   C. It is formed by the catabolism of food.
   D. All of the above are true.

8. Edema may result from which of the following?
   A. Retention of electrolytes
   B. Decreased blood pressure
   C. Increased concentration of blood plasma proteins
   D. All of the above

9. The most abundant and most important positive plasma ion is which of the following?
   A. Sodium
   B. Chloride
   C. Calcium
   D. Oxygen

10. Which of the following is true when extracellular fluid volume decreases?
    A. Aldosterone secretion increases.
    B. Kidney tubule reabsorption of sodium increases.
    C. Urine volume decreases.
    D. All of the above are true.

Completion

Choose from the words below to complete the following statements. Write the corresponding letter in the answer blank.

A. Aldosterone	F. Electrolytes	K. Plasma
B. Edema	G. Positive	L. Urine
C. Proteins	H. Antidiuretic hormone	M. Interstitial fluid
D. Decreases	I. Dehydration	N. Fluid balance
E. Diuretic	J. Extracellular fluid	

11. Any drug that promotes or stimulates the production of urine is called a _____.

12. The presence of abnormally large amounts of fluid in the intercellular tissue spaces of the body is called _____.

13. Water located outside of cells is called _____. It can be divided into two categories. If located in the spaces between the cells, it is called _____; and if located in blood vessels, it is called _____.

14. Compounds such as sodium chloride that form ions when placed in solution are called _____.

15. When the adrenal cortex increases its secretion of aldosterone, urine volume _____.

16. Most fluids leave the body in the form of _____.

17. When fluid output is greater than fluid intake, _____ occurs.

18. How much water moves into blood from interstitial fluid depends largely on the concentration of _____ present in blood plasma. These substances act as a water-pulling or water-holding force.

19. Urine volume is regulated primarily by a hormone secreted by the posterior lobe of the pituitary gland called _____ and by a hormone secreted by the adrenal gland called _____.

20. Homeostasis of fluids is also known as _____.

APPLYING WHAT YOU KNOW

47. Holly is pregnant and experienced repeated vomiting episodes throughout the day for several days in a row. Her doctor became concerned, admitted her to the hospital, and began intravenous administrations of normal saline. How will this help Holly?

48. Cara has a minor bladder infection. She has heard that this is often the result of the urine being less acidic than necessary and that she should drink cranberry juice to correct the acid problem. She has no cranberry juice, so she decides to substitute orange juice. Why would this substitution not be effective in correcting the acid problem?

49. Mr. Shearer has frequent bouts of hyperacidity of the stomach. Which will assist in neutralizing the acid more promptly: milk or milk of magnesia?

50. Word Find

Find and circle 18 terms presented in this chapter. Words may be spelled top to bottom, bottom to top, right to left, left to right, or diagonally.

```
S I S A T S O E M O H P R G
E C N A L A B D I U L F E F
T S Y E N D I K W T I K A J
Y D M N D E J W L P T D J I
L D N O L H V W O U H D O I
O V E R H Y D R A T I O N S
R E I E E D E M A U R O R Q
T L M T C R U L R F S E O Y
C C U S Z A W E K A T N I X
E O Z O T T T A N A U N M F
L F K D P I O I W W Q L G Q
E N I L C O O H O W S B X S
N J X A L N F S U N L J J J
O C U V S A L G T I S C Z X
N I Z L L D Y X Q Q K D C D
```

ADH	Edema	Nonelectrolytes
Aldosterone	Electrolytes	Output
Anions	Fluid balance	Overhydration
Cations	Homeostasis	Sodium
Dehydration	Intake	Thirst
Diuretic	Kidneys	Water

KNOW YOUR MEDICAL TERMS

Fill in the medical term from the literal translation.

51. Sour/condition _____

52. Two/coal/oxygen _____

53. Acetone/chemical _____

54. Cushion/agent _____

55. Coal/relating to (1) _____ without/water/enzyme (2) _____ (2 words)

56. Ashes/condition _____

▶ *If you had difficulty with this section, review page 574.*

DID YOU KNOW?

- During the nineteenth century, English ships that were at sea for many months at a time carried limes onboard to feed the sailors to protect them from developing scurvy. American ships carried cranberries for this purpose.

ACID-BASE BALANCE

Fill in the crossword puzzle.

ACROSS

1. Acid-base imbalance
3. Vomitus
6. Substance with a pH higher than 7.0
7. Prevents a sharp change in the pH of fluids
8. Released as a waste product from working muscles (two words)

DOWN

1. Substance with a pH lower than 7.0
2. Results from excessive metabolism of fats in uncontrolled diabetics (two words)
4. Serious complication of vomiting
5. Most effective regulators of blood pH

CHECK YOUR KNOWLEDGE

Multiple Choice

Circle the correct answer.

1. What happens as blood flows through lung capillaries?
   A. Carbonic acid in blood decreases.
   B. Hydrogen ions in blood decrease.
   C. Blood pH increases from venous to arterial blood.
   D. All of the above are true.

2. Which of the following organs is considered the most effective regulator of blood carbonic acid levels?
   A. Kidneys
   B. Intestines
   C. Lungs
   D. Stomach

3. Which of the following organs is considered the most effective regulator of blood pH?
   A. Kidneys
   B. Intestines
   C. Lungs
   D. Stomach

4. What is the pH of the blood?
   A. 7.00 to 8.00
   B. 6.25 to 7.45
   C. 7.65 to 7.85
   D. 7.35 to 7.45

5. If the ratio of sodium bicarbonate to carbonate ions is lowered (perhaps 10 to 1) and blood pH is also lowered, what is the condition called?
   A. Uncompensated metabolic acidosis
   B. Uncompensated metabolic alkalosis
   C. Compensated metabolic acidosis
   D. Compensated metabolic alkalosis

6. If a person hyperventilates for an extended time, which of the following will probably develop?
   A. Metabolic acidosis
   B. Metabolic alkalosis
   C. Respiratory acidosis
   D. Respiratory alkalosis

7. What happens when lactic acid dissociates in the blood?
   A. H^+ is added to blood.
   B. pH is lowered.
   C. Acidosis results.
   D. All of the above happen.

8. Which of the following is true of metabolic alkalosis?
   A. It occurs in the case of prolonged vomiting.
   B. It results when the bicarbonate ion is present in excess.
   C. Therapy includes intravenous administration of normal saline.
   D. All of the above are true.

9. Which of the following is a characteristic of a buffer system in the body?
   A. It prevents drastic changes from occurring in body pH.
   B. It picks up both hydrogen and hydroxide ions.
   C. It is exemplified by the bicarbonate-carbonic acid system.
   D. All of the above are true.

10. In the presence of a strong acid (HCl), which of the following is true?
   A. Sodium bicarbonate will react to produce carbonic acid + sodium chloride.
   B. Sodium bicarbonate will react to produce more sodium bicarbonate.
   C. Carbonic acid will react to produce sodium bicarbonate.
   D. Carbonic acid will react to form more carbonic acid.

Matching

Match each description in column A with its corresponding term in column B. (Only one answer is correct for each.)

Column A

_____ 11. pH lower than 7.0

_____ 12. pH higher than 7.0

_____ 13. Prevent sharp pH changes

_____ 14. Decrease in respirations

_____ 15. Increase in respirations

_____ 16. Bicarbonate deficit

_____ 17. Bicarbonate excess

_____ 18. "Fixed" acid

_____ 19. Enzyme found in red blood cells

_____ 20. Lower-than-normal ratio of sodium bicarbonate to carbonic acid

Column B

A. Metabolic acidosis

B. Metabolic alkalosis

C. Alkaline solution

D. Lactic acid

E. Respiratory acidosis

F. Respiratory alkalosis

G. Acidic solution

H. Uncompensated metabolic acidosis

I. Buffers

J. Carbonic anhydrase

Match the two hormones below to their corresponding descriptions. Write the letter in the answer blank.

A. FSH   B. LH

_____ 95. Ovulating hormone

_____ 96. Secreted during first days of menstrual cycle

_____ 97. Secreted after estrogen level of blood increases

_____ 98. Causes final maturation of follicle and ovum

_____ 99. Suppressed by birth control pills

▷ *If you had difficulty with this section, review pages 607-609.*

DISORDERS OF THE FEMALE REPRODUCTIVE SYSTEM

Match each numbered description to its corresponding disease or condition. Write the letter in the answer blank.

_____ 100. Often occurs as a result of an STD or a "yeast infection"

_____ 101. Benign tumor of smooth muscle and fibrous connective tissue; also known as a *fibroid tumor*

_____ 102. Yeast infection characterized by leukorrhea

_____ 103. Inflammation of an ovary

_____ 104. Benign lumps in one or both breasts

_____ 105. Venereal diseases

_____ 106. Results from pathogenic organisms transmitted from another person; for example, an STD

_____ 107. Painful menstruation

_____ 108. Asymptomatic in most women and nearly all men

_____ 109. Results from a hormonal imbalance rather than from an infection or disease condition

_____ 110. Screening test for cervical cancer

_____ 111. Causes blisters on the skin of the genitals; the blisters may disappear temporarily, but recur, especially as a result of stress

A. Candidiasis

B. Dysmenorrhea

C. Exogenous infections

D. DUB

E. Myoma

F. Vaginitis

G. Sexually transmitted diseases (STDs)

H. Oophoritis

I. Fibrocystic disease

J. Pap smear

K. Genital herpes

L. Trichomoniasis

▷ *If you had difficulty with this section, review pages 609-616.*

UNSCRAMBLE THE WORDS

112. **U L A V V**

113. **T S T S E E**

114. **M N S S E E**

115. **A I E I F M B R**

116. **C U E R P P E**

Take the circled letters, unscramble them, and fill in the solution.

Where Kathleen displayed the flowers from her husband.

117.

APPLYING WHAT YOU KNOW

118. Sam is going into the hospital for the surgical removal of his testes. As a result of this surgery, will Sam be impotent?

119. When baby Christopher was born, the pediatrician, Dr. Self, discovered that his left testicle had not descended into the scrotum. If this situation is not corrected soon, might baby Christopher be sterile or impotent?

120. Harlean contracted gonorrhea. By the time she made an appointment to see her doctor, it had spread to her abdominal organs. How is this possible when gonorrhea is a disease of the reproductive system?

121. Dr. Sullivan advises Mrs. Harlan to have a bilateral oophorectomy. Is this a sterilization procedure? Will she experience menopause?

122. Vicki had a total hysterectomy. Will she experience menopause?

123. Word Find

Find and circle 18 terms presented in this chapter. Words may be spelled top to bottom, bottom to top, right to left, left to right, or diagonally.

```
M  K  O  V  I  D  U  C  T  S  E  D  H  G
S  E  I  R  A  V  O  I  F  U  T  G  L  L
I  N  H  Z  H  M  P  M  K  O  H  I  C  W
D  D  V  A  S  D  E  F  E  R  E  N  S  H
I  O  A  C  C  I  P  J  V  E  H  Y  D  S
H  M  G  R  R  B  M  N  X  F  G  Y  I  O
C  E  I  O  O  E  Z  Y  T  I  C  S  T  E
R  T  N  S  T  P  S  D  D  N  O  V  A  D
O  R  A  O  U  W  E  B  A  I  J  S  M  Z
T  I  C  M  M  E  Y  N  E  M  D  L  R  V
P  U  A  E  U  D  G  M  I  E  H  I  E  H
Y  M  O  T  C  E  T  A  T  S  O  R  P  B
R  P  E  E  R  M  N  E  G  O  R  T  S  E
C  O  W  P  E  R  S  I  N  X  K  E  A  P
```

Acrosome	Meiosis	Scrotum
Cowpers	Ovaries	Seminiferous
Cryptorchidism	Oviducts	Sperm
Endometrium	Penis	Spermatids
Epididymis	Pregnancy	Vagina
Estrogen	Prostatectomy	Vas deferens

KNOW YOUR MEDICAL TERMS

Identify the medical term from the literal translation.

124. body/yellow/thing _____

125. within/womb/thing _____

126. offspring/relating to _____

127. lips/large _____

128. months _____

129. egg/cell _____

130. seed _____

131. tunic or coat/white _____

132. within/womb/condition _____

133. painful/month/flow _____

134. not/fruitful/state _____

135. white/flow _____

136. pubic region/cut/action _____

137. vessel/out/cut/action _____

138. tube/inflammation _____

▶ *If you had difficulty with this section, review pages 590-592.*

DID YOU KNOW?

- The testes produce approximately 50 million sperm per day. Every 2 to 3 months they produce enough cells to populate the entire earth.
- There are an estimated 925,000 daily occurrences of STD transmission and 550,000 daily conceptions worldwide.
- The United States has one of the highest teen pregnancy rates of all industrialized nations. Rates in France, Germany, and Japan are four times lower.
- All babies have blue eyes when they are born. Melanin and ultraviolet exposure light are needed to bring out the true color of a baby's eyes.

REPRODUCTIVE SYSTEMS

Fill in the crossword puzzle.

ACROSS

2. Female erectile tissue
3. Colored area around nipple
5. Male reproductive fluid
6. Sex cells
7. External genitalia
10. Male sex hormone

DOWN

1. Failure to have a menstrual period
2. Surgical removal of foreskin
4. Foreskin
8. Menstrual period
9. Essential organs of reproduction

UNSCRAMBLE THE WORDS

62. **A N N F C Y I**

63. **N A A L T T S O P**

64. **O G S S N E G R A O N E I**

65. **G T E Y Z O**

66. **H D O O L H C I D**

Take the circled letters, unscramble them, and fill in the solution.

The secret to Farmer Brown's prize pumpkin crop.

67.

APPLYING WHAT YOU KNOW

68. Billy's mother told the pediatrician during his 1-year visit that Billy had tripled his birth weight, was crawling actively, and could stand alone. Is Billy's development normal, retarded, or advanced?

69. John is 70 years old. He has always enjoyed food and has had a hearty appetite. Lately, however, he has complained that food "just doesn't taste as good anymore." What might be a possible explanation?

70. Mr. Gaylor has noticed hearing problems but only under certain circumstances. He has difficulty with certain tones, especially high or low tones, but has no problem with everyday conversation. What might be a possible explanation?

71. Mrs. Lowell gave birth to twin girls. The obstetrician, Dr. Sullivan, advised Mr. Lowell that even though the girls looked identical, they were really fraternal twins. How was he able to deduce this?

72. Word Find

Find and circle 13 terms presented in this chapter. Words may be spelled top to bottom, bottom to top, right to left, left to right, or diagonally.

```
F  C  M  P  O  D  N  P  P  A  G  M  J  N  Z
K  E  C  N  E  C  S  E  L  O  D  A  G  G  M
I  N  R  B  U  X  T  K  D  A  Y  Q  T  F  R
L  D  L  T  O  M  S  D  W  A  E  Z  B  F  E
Z  O  B  A  I  S  P  M  A  L  C  E  E  R  P
W  D  I  M  P  L  A  N  T  A  T  I  O  N  L
H  E  N  M  K  A  I  T  E  P  D  K  S  X  A
W  R  G  A  S  A  R  Z  R  N  T  Q  P  Y  C
L  M  Q  S  I  J  O  O  A  U  B  F  G  T  E
R  T  N  T  B  N  G  E  S  T  A  T  I  O  N
L  A  T  I  N  E  G  N  O  C  I  T  F  Z  T
D  C  B  T  R  L  A  S  G  C  O  O  R  R  A
E  N  O  I  T  I  R  U  T  R  A  P  N  S  B
N  V  A  S  N  N  E  G  O  T  A  R  E  T  E
```

Adolescence	Implantation	Placenta
Congenital	Laparoscope	Preeclampsia
Endoderm	Mastitis	Progeria
Fertilization	Parturition	Teratogen
Gestation		

KNOW YOUR MEDICAL TERMS

Indicate whether the medical term is the correct one for the given literal translation by T (true) or F (false).

_____ 73. Adolescence   (grow up/state)

_____ 74. Ectoderm   (outside/skin)

_____ 75. Gestation   (time/deliver)

_____ 76. Neonate   (new/born)

_____ 77. Zygote   (little/egg)

_____ 78. Menopause   (month/cease)

_____ 79. Placenta   (flat/cake)

_____ 80. Glaucoma   (cloud/tumor)

▷ *If you had difficulty with this section, review pages 624 and 625.*

DID YOU KNOW?

• Brain cells do not regenerate. One beer permanently destroys 10,000 brain cells.

GROWTH AND DEVELOPMENT

Fill in the crossword puzzle.

ACROSS

7. Old age
9. Fatty deposit buildup on walls of arteries
10. Cloudy lens
11. Name of zygote after 3 days
12. Fertilized ovum

DOWN

1. Process of birth
2. Science of the development of the individual before birth
3. Study of how germ layers develop into tissues
4. Name of zygote after implantation
5. First 4 weeks of infancy
6. Hardening of the lens
8. Eye disease marked by increased pressure in the eyeball
10. Will develop into a fetal membrane in the placenta

CHECK YOUR KNOWLEDGE

Multiple Choice

Circle the correct answer.

1. When the human embryo is a hollow ball of cells consisting of an outer cell layer and an inner cell mass, what is it called?
   A. Morula
   B. Chorion
   C. Blastocyst
   D. Zygote

2. Degenerative changes in the urinary system that accompany old age include which of the following?
   A. Decreased capacity of the bladder and the inability to empty or void completely
   B. Decrease in the number of nephrons
   C. Less blood flow through the kidneys
   D. All of the above

3. The frontal and maxillary sinuses of the facial region acquire permanent placement or develop fully when the individual is in a stage of development known as which of the following?
   A. Infancy
   B. Childhood
   C. Adolescence
   D. Adulthood

4. The first 4 weeks of human life following birth are referred to as which of the following?
   A. Neonatal
   B. Infancy
   C. Prenatal
   D. Embryonic

5. Which statement regarding labor is *not* true?
   A. It usually lasts from 6 to 24 hours.
   B. Expulsion of the placenta is considered part of the labor process.
   C. There are 3 stages of labor.
   D. A breech birth usually goes through the same stages but requires a slightly longer labor period.

6. Which of the following is characteristic of the disorder called *presbyopia*?
   A. It is very characteristic of old age.
   B. It causes farsightedness in some individuals.
   C. It is characterized by the lens in the eye becoming hard and losing its elasticity.
   D. All of the above are true.

7. The three most important "low-tech" methods for improving the quality of life as you age are:
   A. Healthy diet, exercise, and stress management
   B. A healthy diet, marriage, and money
   C. A healthy diet, good job, and living in the suburbs
   D. A healthy diet, weight management, and exercise

8. Which of the following events, if any, is *not* characteristic of adolescence?
   A. Bone closure occurs.
   B. Secondary sexual characteristics develop.
   C. Very rapid growth occurs.
   D. Growth spurts occur in both sexes.

9. Which of the following events is *not* characteristic of the prenatal period of development?
   A. Blastocyst is formed.
   B. Histogenesis occurs.
   C. Bone closure occurs.
   D. Amniotic cavity is formed.

10. Which of the following structures is derived from ectoderm?
   A. The lining of the lungs
   B. The brain
   C. The kidneys
   D. All of the above

CHAPTER 25

Genetics and Genetic Diseases

L ook around your classroom and you will notice various combinations of hair color, eye color, body size, skin tone, hair texture, gender, etc. Everyone has unique body features and this phenomenon alerts us to the marvel of genetics. Independent units, called *genes*, are responsible for the inheritance of biological traits. Genes determine the structure and function of the human body by producing specific regulatory enzymes. Some genes are dominant and some are recessive. Dominant genes produce traits that appear in the offspring and recessive genes have traits that do not appear in the offspring when they are masked by a dominant gene.

Gene therapy is one of the latest advances of science. This revolutionary branch of medicine combines current technology with genetic research to unlock the secrets of the human body. Daily discoveries in the prevention, diagnosis, treatment, and cure of diseases and disorders are being revealed as a result of genetic therapy. Knowledge of genetics is necessary to understand the basic mechanism by which traits are transmitted from parents to offspring.

TOPICS FOR REVIEW

Your review of this chapter should include an understanding of chromosomes, genes, and gene expression. You should continue your study with a knowledge of common genetic diseases. Finally, your review should conclude with an understanding of the prevention and treatment of genetic diseases.

GENETICS AND HUMAN DISEASE

CHROMOSOMES AND GENES

HUMAN GENOME

Match each term on the left with its corresponding description on the right. Write the letter in the answer blank.

_____ 1. Gene	A.	DNA molecule
_____ 2. Chromosome	B.	Male or female reproductive cell
_____ 3. Gamete	C.	Special form of nuclear division
_____ 4. Meiosis	D.	Formed by union of sperm and ovum at conception
_____ 5. Zygote	E.	Distinct code within a DNA molecule
_____ 6. Genome	F.	Adenine
_____ 7. Genomics	G.	Entire collection of genetic material in each typical cell
_____ 8. Proteomics	H.	Cartoon of a chromosome
_____ 9. Ideogram	I.	Analysis of the genome's code
_____ 10. Nucleotide base	J.	Analysis of the proteins encoded by the genome

▶ *If you had difficulty with this section, review pages 648-653.*

GENE EXPRESSION

Fill in the blanks.

After experimentation with pea plants, Mendel discovered that each inherited trait is controlled by two sets of similar (11) _____, one from each parent. He also noted that some genes are (12) _____ and some are (13) _____.
In the example of albinism, a person with the gene combination of Aa is said to be a genetic

(14) _____. If two different dominant genes occur together a form of

dominance called (15) _____ exists.

(16) _____ chromosomes do not have matching structures. If an individual has the sex chromosomes XX, that person will have the sexual characteristics of a

(17) _____. (18) _____ simply means

"change." A (19) _____ _____ is a change in the genetic code.

▶ *If you had difficulty with this section, review pages 653-656.*

GENETIC DISEASES

Match each description on the left with its corresponding term on the right. Write the letter in the answer blank.

_____ 20. Caused by recessive genes in chromosome pair 7

_____ 21. Results in total blindness by age 30

_____ 22. Disease conditions that result from the combined effects of inheritance and environmental factors

_____ 23. Results from a failure to produce the enzyme phenylalanine hydroxylase

_____ 24. Presence of only one autosome instead of a pair

_____ 25. Usually caused by trisomy of chromosome 21

_____ 26. Cystic fibrosis is an example

_____ 27. Results from nondisjunction of chromosomes and typically has the XXY pattern

_____ 28. Term used to describe what happens when a pair of chromosomes fails to separate

_____ 29. Sometimes called *XO syndrome*, it is treated with hormone therapy

A. Single-gene disease
B. Nondisjunction
C. Monosomy
D. Leber hereditary optic neuropathy
E. Cystic fibrosis
F. Phenylketonuria
G. Down syndrome
H. Klinefelter syndrome
I. Turner syndrome
J. Genetic predisposition

▶ *If you had difficulty with this section, review pages 656-660.*

PREVENTION AND TREATMENT OF GENETIC DISEASES

Circle the correct answer.

30. A pedigree is a chart that can be used to determine:
    A. Genetic relationships in a family over several generations
    B. The possibility of producing offspring with certain genetic disorders
    C. The possibility of a person developing a genetic disorder late in life
    D. All of the above
    E. None of the above

31. The Punnett square is a grid used to determine:
    A. Genetic disorders
    B. The probability of inheriting genetic traits
    C. Proper gene replacement therapy
    D. The necessity for amniocentesis

32. Some forms of cancer are thought to be caused, at least in part, by abnormal genes called:
    A. Cancercytes
    B. Trisomy
    C. Oncogenes
    D. Autosomes

33. When producing a karyotype, the most common source of cells for the sample is the:
    A. Vagina
    B. Rectum
    C. Lining of the cheek
    D. Throat

34. An ultrasound transducer is used during amniocentesis to:
    A. Create a sharper image
    B. Take measurements during the procedure
    C. Prevent damaging rays during the procedure
    D. Guide the tip of the needle to prevent placental damage

35. Electrophoresis is a process that:
    A. Provides a method for DNA analysis
    B. Means electric separation
    C. Is the basis for DNA fingerprinting
    D. All of the above

36. The use of genetic therapy began in 1990 with a group of young children who had:
    A. AIDS
    B. Adenosine deaminase deficiency
    C. Hemophilia
    D. Cystic fibrosis

True or False

If the statement is true, write "T" in the answer blank. If the statement is false, correct the statement by circling the incorrect term and writing the correct term in the answer blank.

_____ 37. Chorionic villus sampling is a procedure in which cells that surround a young embryo are collected through the opening of the cervix.

_____ 38. Karyotyping is the process used for DNA fingerprinting.

_____ 39. In amniocentesis, normal genes are introduced with the hope that they will add to the production of the needed protein.

_____ 40. Deficiency of adenosine deaminase results in severe combined immune deficiency.

_____ 41. One hypothesis that may explain some forms of cancer is known as the *tumor suppressor gene* hypothesis.

▶ *If you had difficulty with this section, review pages 660-666.*

UNSCRAMBLE THE WORDS

42. **R C R R I E A**

43. **Y T S M O I R**

44. **E G N E**

45. **D P E R E G I E**

46. **S O E M C R O S H O M**

Take the circled letters, unscramble them, and fill in the solution.

How Bill made his fortune.

47.

APPLYING WHAT YOU KNOW

48. Steve's mother has a dominant gene for dark skin color. Steve's father has a dominant gene for light skin color. What color will Steve's skin most likely be?

49. Mr. and Mrs. Freund both carry recessive genes for cystic fibrosis. Using your knowledge of the Punnett square, estimate the probability of one of their offspring inheriting this condition.

50. Meredith is pregnant and is over 40. She fears her age may predispose her baby to genetic disorders and she has sought the advice of a genetic counselor. What tests might the counselor suggest to alleviate Meredith's fears?

51. Punnett Square

Fill in the Punnett square for the following genetic cases:

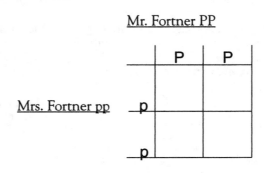

Mr. Fortner has two dominant genes for brown eyes and Mrs. Fortner has two recessive genes for blue eyes.

    A. The offspring of Mr. and Mrs. Fortner have a _____ % chance of having brown eyes and a

        _____ % chance of having blue eyes.

    B. Will Mr. and Mrs. Fortner's offspring be carriers of blue eyes?

    C. If Mr. and Mrs. Fortner's offspring mates with another offspring who is a carrier of blue eyes, what is the probability of the resulting offspring having blue eyes?

Draw your own Punnett square to determine your answer.

Mrs. Harrington Pp

		P	p
Mr. Harrington Pp	**P**		
	p		

Mr. and Mrs. Harrington are both carriers for albinism. Using the Punnett square, determine what percentage of Mr. and Mrs. Harrington's offspring will:

    A. Have normal pigmentation _____

    B. Be carriers _____

    C. Have albinism _____

52.   Word Find

Find and circle 14 terms presented in this chapter. Words may be spelled top to bottom, bottom to top, right to left, left to right, or diagonally.

Amniocentesis	Hemophilia
Carrier	Karyotype
Chromosomes	Meiosis
Codominance	Monosomy
DNA	Nondisjunction
Gametes	Recessive
Gene therapy	Zygote

```
N  J  A  T  E  T  O  G  Y  Z  S  F  I  H  Q
M  O  M  D  P  S  I  W  P  L  I  K  Y  E  K
S  M  N  P  E  E  F  Y  A  Z  S  A  X  M  C
F  A  I  D  V  M  M  Z  R  Z  O  R  P  O  L
H  R  O  J  I  O  E  U  E  I  I  Y  D  P  O
I  Q  C  M  S  S  O  L  H  Z  E  O  G  H  X
Y  J  E  O  S  O  J  Z  T  W  M  T  D  I  Q
G  E  N  I  E  M  C  U  E  I  E  Y  X  L  Q
A  O  T  G  C  O  P  K  N  E  J  P  I  I  G
M  P  E  M  E  R  D  A  E  C  P  E  J  A  I
E  D  S  I  R  H  N  C  G  B  T  Z  P  S  Y
T  G  I  D  U  C  G  C  P  X  H  I  F  G  X
E  W  S  R  E  I  R  R  A  C  V  I  O  H  S
S  W  V  B  K  R  C  R  Y  B  V  U  C  N  S
```

KNOW YOUR MEDICAL TERMS

Select the letters that represent the literal translation of the word. Use as many letters as necessary.

a. white
b. single
c. self
d. relating to
e. sexual union
f. gene
g. birth membrane

h. process
i. nucleus
j. retreat
k. idea
l. body
m. characterized by
n. change

o. state
p. kind
q. entire collection
r. prick
s. produce
t. drawing

_____ 53. Autosome

_____ 54. Gamete

_____ 55. Genome

_____ 56. Recessive

_____ 57. Albinism

_____ 58. Amniocentesis

_____ 59. Ideogram

_____ 60. Monosomy

_____ 61. Mutagen

_____ 62. Karyotype

▶ *If you had difficulty with this section, review page 650.*

DID YOU KNOW?

- Scientists now believe the human body has 50,000 to 100,000 genes packed into just 46 chromosomes.
- If you could unwrap the entire DNA sequence you have in your cells, you could reach the moon 6000 times.
- If the human genome was a book, it would be equivalent to 800 dictionaries.
- Human DNA is 96% identical to chimpanzee DNA.

GENETICS

Fill in the crossword puzzle.

ACROSS

2. Name for the 22 pairs of matched chromosomes
3. Lack of melanin in the skin and eyes
6. Refers to genes that appear in the offspring
7. Chart that illustrates genetic relationships in a family over several generations
8. All genetic material in each cell
9. Scientific study of inheritance

DOWN

1. Trisomy 21 (two words)
4. Agents that cause genetic mutations
5. Triplet of autosomes rather than a pair
7. Excess of phenylketone in the urine (abbreviation)

CHECK YOUR KNOWLEDGE

Multiple Choice

Circle the correct answer.

1. Independent assortment of chromosomes ensures:
   A. Each offspring from a single set of parents is genetically unique
   B. At meiosis, each gamete receives the same number of chromosomes
   C. That the sex chromosomes always match
   D. An equal number of males and females are born

2. Which of the following statements is *not* true of a pedigree?
   A. They are useful to genetic counselors in predicting the possibility of producing offspring with genetic disorders.
   B. They may allow a person to determine his likelihood of developing a genetic disorder later in life.
   C. They indicate the occurrence of those family members affected by a trait, as well as carriers of the trait.
   D. All of the above are true of a pedigree.

3. The genes that cause albinism are:
   A. Codominant
   B. Dominant
   C. Recessive
   D. AA

4. During meiosis, matching pairs of chromosomes line up and exchange genes from their location to the same location on the other side; a process called:
   A. Gene linkage
   B. Crossing-over
   C. Cross-linkage
   D. Genetic variation

5. When a sperm cell unites with an ovum, a _____ is formed.
   A. Zygote
   B. Chromosome
   C. Gamete
   D. None of the above

6. DNA molecules can also be called:
   A. A chromatin strand
   B. A chromosome
   C. A and B
   D. None of the above

7. Nonsexual traits:
   A. Show up more often in females than in males
   B. May be carried on sex chromosomes
   C. Are the result of genetic mutation
   D. All of the above

8. If a person has only X chromosomes, that person is:
   A. Missing essential proteins
   B. Abnormal
   C. Female
   D. Male

9. A karyotype:
   A. Can detect trisomy
   B. Is useful for diagnosing a tubal pregnancy
   C. Is frequently used as a tool in gene augmentation therapy
   D. Can detect the presence of oncogenes

10. Which of the following pairs is mismatched?
    A. SCID—gene therapy
    B. Turner syndrome—trisomy
    C. PKU—recessive
    D. Cystic fibrosis—single-gene disease

Completion

Complete the following statements using the terms listed below. Write the corresponding letter in the answer blank.

A. Cystic fibrosis
B. Males
C. Phenylketonuria
D. Carrier
E. Genome
F. Females

G. Pedigree
H. Oncogenes
I. Karyotype
J. Tay-Sachs disease
K. Amniocentesis
L. Hemophilia

11. Abnormal genes called _____ are believed to be related to cancer.

12. Fetal tissue may be collected by a procedure called _____.

13. An abnormal accumulation of phenylalanine results in _____.

14. The entire collection of genetic material in each cell is called the _____.

15. _____ is caused by recessive genes in chromosome pair seven.

16. A _____ is a chart that illustrates genetic relationships over several generations.

17. A _____ is a person who has a recessive gene that is not expressed.

18. Absence of an essential lipid-producing enzyme may result in the recessive condition _____.

19. _____ is a recessive X-linked disorder.

20. Klinefelter syndrome occurs in _____.